GUATEMALA CITY & ANTIGUA

AL ARGUETA

Contents

Guatemala City & Antigua

Guatemala City

Look for ★ to find recommended
sights, activities, dining, and lodging.

Highlights

★ **Palacio Nacional de la Cultura:** At the heart of downtown Guatemala City, this former presidential palace now serves as a museum that offers a fascinating glimpse into the country's rich history (page 17).

★ **Zona Viva:** Guatemala City's most cosmopolitan sector, while offering some of the city's best hotels, is also a fun place for a meal and a night on the town (page 28).

★ **Museo Ixchel:** The city's finest museum is a wonderful tribute to Mayan culture and to Guatemala's famous textiles and traditional village attire (page 29).

★ **Museo Miraflores:** This excellent museum is dedicated to the ancient Mayan site of Kaminaljuyú, which occupied the valley in which Guatemala City now stands. Several of the site's temple mounds lie nearby (page 29).

★ **Museo Nacional de Arqueología y Etnología:** Before or after visiting Guatemala's fascinating Mayan sites, head to this museum to admire many of the original pieces once found there, including beautifully carved monuments and brilliant jade masks (page 30).

Due to its much-maligned international image, you'll probably be surprised when you first lay eyes on Guatemala City from the window of your airplane. Even if you've visited other Central American capitals, you'll be taken

by Guatemala City's beauty from the air. Bordered by a lake, forested mountains, and four volcanoes, the nation's capital is a bustling urban agglomeration of three million inhabitants occupying a broad valley and spilling into ravines and neighboring hillsides.

The beauty of its physical surroundings aside, Guatemala City, or "Guate," as it's more commonly called by locals, can seem polluted, noisy, and downright dodgy once you step onto its streets—however, the same can be said of New York or Mexico City. It's all a matter of getting acquainted with your surroundings and discovering the pleasant aspects of this mountain city. Among these are a temperate spring-like climate, a splendid scenic backdrop, excellent dining and entertainment options, and the opportunity to travel in relative comfort with all of the amenities of a cosmopolitan city.

If you give it a chance, you'll find that Guate grows on you after a while. As far as

Latin American capitals go, you could certainly do worse. (Some travelers find other Central American capitals less agreeable.) As the region's largest and most cosmopolitan city, Guatemala City has a wide variety of accommodations and entertainment options suited to tastes, needs, and budget.

The remodeled La Aurora International Airport serves as a fitting gateway to Central America's largest city. Just minutes from the airport, you'll find most of the areas frequented by Guatemala's well-to-do and expat residents. Scattered among forest-clad ravines and sprawling east into neighboring mountainsides are Guatemala City's business, retail, and residential sectors. The northern part of the city is home to its downtown core, which has unfortunately seen better days as a colonial capital, but is also the ongoing focus of some much-needed urban renewal. Tumbling out into surrounding ravines and plateaus in the vicinity of the downtown core

Previous: Guatemala City's Zona 14; aerial view of Guatemala City's older districts. **Above:** Hard Rock Café Guatemala City.

Guatemala City

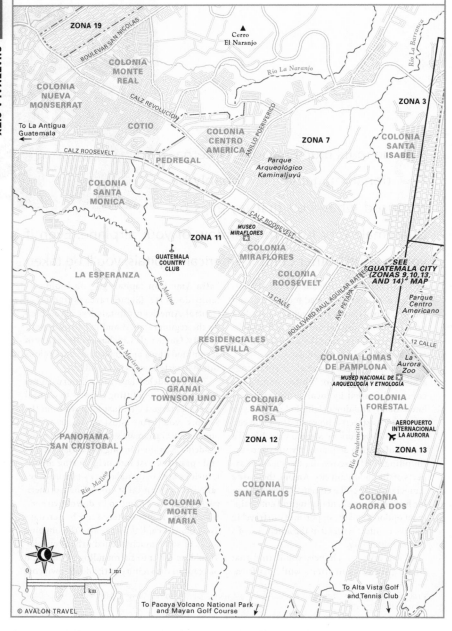

ZONA 19

BOULEVAR SAN NICOLAS

▲ Cerro
El Naranjo

COLONIA
MONTE
REAL

Río La Naranjo

COLONIA
NUEVA
MONSERRAT

CALZ REVOLUCIÓN

ZONA 3

To La Antigua
Guatemala
←

COTIO

CALZ ROOSEVELT

PEDREGAL

COLONIA
CENTRO
AMERICA

ANILLO PERIFÉRICO

ZONA 7

COLONIA
SANTA
ISABEL

Río La Barranca

Parque
Arqueológico
Kaminaljuyú

COLONIA
SANTA
MONICA

CALZ ROOSEVELT

MUSEO
MIRAFLORES

ZONA 11

GUATEMALA
COUNTRY
CLUB

COLONIA
MIRAFLORES

LA ESPERANZA

Río Molino

COLONIA
ROOSEVELT

13 CALLE

BOULEVARD RAUL AGUILAR BATRES

AVE. PETAPA

SEE
"GUATEMALA CITY
(ZONAS 9, 10, 13,
AND 14)" MAP

Parque
Centro
Americano

RESIDENCIALES
SEVILLA

Río Marioval

COLONIA
GRANAI
TOWNSON UNO

COLONIA LOMAS
DE PAMPLONA

12 CALLE

La
Aurora
Zoo

MUSEO NACIONAL DE
ARQUEOLOGÍA Y ETNOLOGÍA

COLONIA
SANTA
ROSA

COLONIA
FORESTAL

PANORAMA
SAN CRISTOBAL

Río Molino

ZONA 12

Río Guadroncito

AEROPUERTO
INTERNACIONAL
✈ LA AURORA

ZONA 13

COLONIA
MONTE
MARIA

COLONIA
SAN CARLOS

COLONIA
AORORA DOS

0   1 mi

0   1 km

© AVALON TRAVEL

To Pacaya Volcano National Park
and Mayan Golf Course ↓

To Alta Vista Golf
and Tennis Club

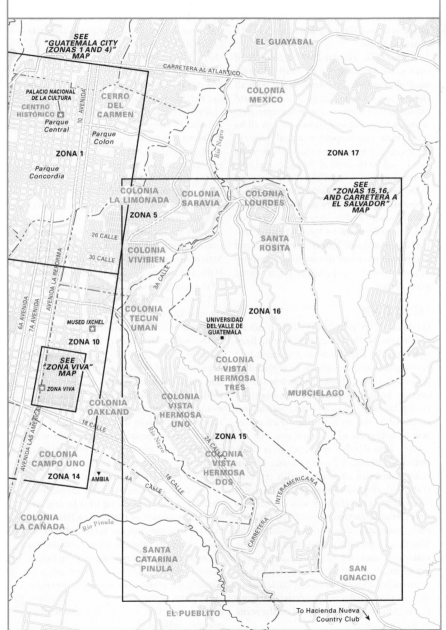

SEE
"GUATEMALA CITY
(ZONAS 1 AND 4)"
MAP

EL GUAYABAL

CARRETERA AL ATLANTICO

PALACIO NACIONAL
DE LA CULTURA

CENTRO
HISTÓRICO ✚

CERRO
DEL
CARMEN

COLONIA
MEXICO

Parque
Central

Parque
Colon

Río Negro

ZONA 1

ZONA 17

Parque
Concordia

SEE
"ZONAS 15,16,
AND CARRETERA A
EL SALVADOR"
MAP

COLONIA
LA LIMONADA

COLONIA
SARAVIA

COLONIA
LOURDES

ZONA 5

26 CALLE

SANTA
ROSITA

30 CALLE

COLONIA
VIVIBIEN

AVENIDA LA REFORMA

3A CALLE

COLONIA
TECUN
UMAN

ZONA 16

6A AVENIDA

7A AVENIDA

MUSEO IXCHEL ✚

UNIVERSIDAD
DEL VALLE DE
GUATEMALA ■

ZONA 10

COLONIA
VISTA
HERMOSA
TRES

MURCIELAGO

SEE
"ZONA VIVA"
MAP

✚ ZONA VIVA

COLONIA
OAKLAND

COLONIA
VISTA
HERMOSA
UNO

18 CALLE

Río Negro

ZONA 15

AVENIDA LAS AMÉRICAS

COLONIA
CAMPO UNO

ZONA 14

▼
AMBIA

2A CALLE

COLONIA
VISTA
HERMOSA
DOS

4A CALLE

18 CALLE

INTERAMERICANA

CARRETERA

COLONIA
LA CAÑADA

Río Pinula

SANTA
CATARINA
PINULA

SAN
IGNACIO

EL PUEBLITO

To Hacienda Nueva
Country Club ↘

are the city's slums, while its industrial sectors lie mostly to the south and west. Chances are you won't be venturing into the these two sectors, just as you likely wouldn't hang out in a Brazilian *favela*.

It should be expected that a country of such great wealth (though poorly distributed) should have a modern capital with all the developed world comforts one would expect to find there. Great restaurants, museums, shops, and entertainment can all be found in this cosmopolitan capital. Like everything else in Guatemala, it all coexists side by side with some of the uglier realities. Things can look very different from one *zona* to the next. It's all there for you to see, and nowhere else in the country is this striking contrast of wealth and poverty so evident. Look at a visit to Guatemala City as a glimpse into the nation's culture, history, and politics, and a worthy introduction to a fascinating country of contrasts with unexpected surprises around every corner.

HISTORY

Guatemala City is in fact the fourth capital of Guatemala, the other three having been destroyed by natural disasters, including earthquakes and mudslides, or replaced by the establishment of Spanish-modeled urban centers, as in the case of the first highland capital Iximché. Like Iximché, the land now occupied by the modern-day urban center was once the site of a Mayan city that exercised considerable influence over trade routes for obsidian during Classic Mayan times thanks to an alliance with the central Mexican powerhouse of Teotihuacán. Kaminaljuyú, as the city was called, was first settled sometime around 400 BC. The early foundational cultures preceding the Mayan city established agriculture in the valley now occupied by Guatemala City and settled much of it, mostly in the western part of the valley. As with the other Classic Mayan sites, Kaminaljuyú was just a distant memory by the time the Spanish arrived on the scene in the 16th century.

The city's modern settlement dates to 1776, in the aftermath of the 1773 earthquakes of Santa Marta, which rocked the previous capital, now known as La Antigua Guatemala (The Old Guatemala, or "La Antigua" for short). Debate over whether or not to rebuild La Antigua raged for a few years, but in the end it was decided to start all over again in the neighboring Valle de la Ermita (Valley of the Hermitage), as the valley was known. An edict by Governor Martín Mayorga made the move official. It took a while for the new capital to catch on, as many Antigua residents refused to move despite Spanish decrees ordering the settlement of the new city. In 1800, the population of Guatemala City was only 25,000. The new city was laid out in a grid pattern, much like every other town established by the Spanish, with the construction of major public buildings including the Catedral Metropolitana (cathedral), Cabildo (Town Hall), and Palacio de los Capitanes Generales. Of these, only the cathedral remains standing.

Like its predecessor, Antigua Guatemala, the new Guatemalan capital would experience its own series of destructive earthquakes in December 1917, lasting into February of the following year. By this time, it seems, the population had come to terms with the fact that much of Guatemala lies upon one of the world's most active fault lines. The fault line would again wreak widespread havoc with another earthquake in 1976. Ironically, the most recent earthquake triggered wide-scale migration into the city, resulting in the establishment of many slums lining the city's numerous ravines, or *barrancos*.

The city grew tremendously throughout the 20th century, spreading from its original core (now known as the Centro Histórico) and spilling out into the surrounding *barrancos* and up into the mountains lining the western and eastern edges of the valley. Much of the country's industry is concentrated here, fueling economic migration from other parts of the country. The population of Guatemala City's metro area now reaches over four million.

CLIMATE

Guatemala City enjoys a delightful climate almost year-round. Its location in a valley at an altitude of 1,493 meters (4,897 feet) above sea level ensures that it never gets excessively warm, as do some other, low-lying Central American capitals. This pleasant climate has earned it the nickname "Land of Eternal Spring." It should be noted, however, that the nickname was coined during a long-gone era before the city's exponential growth, which has given rise to urban microclimates such as the urban heat island. The latter is caused when the direct tropical sun heats large expanses of pavement, which in turn heat the surrounding air masses, causing a phenomenon not unlike a large convection oven. The truth is that it can get somewhat hot here during April and May, what locals generally call *verano*, or summer, with daytime highs in the mid- to upper 80s. Longtime residents frequently remark about the increasingly warm summers, which they say have become much warmer than what was once typical. This is also the driest time of year, and the surrounding mountains can turn some rather parched shades of brown. Thermal inversions causing extreme haze are also quite typical this time of year, making Guatemala City look somewhat like a smaller version of Los Angeles. These occur frequently in valleys when a layer of warm air settles over a layer of cooler air lying close to the ground, holding this cooler air down and preventing pollutants from rising and scattering.

Between June and August, after the arrival of the rainy season, mornings are typically sunny and warm, giving way to increasing cloudiness and afternoon showers almost every day. September and October are increasingly rainy with entire stretches of cloudy or rainy days. In November the skies clear and become increasingly windy. Many people equate this time of year with kite-flying, and indeed the giant kite festival in the nearby towns of Sumpango and Sacatepéquez take place on the first of the month. December through February can be chilly here and elsewhere in mountainous parts of Guatemala with the arrival from the north of frequent cold fronts coinciding with the Northern Hemisphere's winter season. Bring some warm clothes if you're traveling to Guatemala City or elsewhere in the highlands during this time of year, as concrete houses with tile floors are the most popular form of architecture and aren't typically heated or carpeted, making it feel even colder.

PLANNING YOUR TIME

Upon international arrival into Guatemala, most travelers eager to make their way to the country's fascinating interior head straight to Antigua Guatemala, taking a shuttle bus from the airport and bypassing Guatemala City altogether. Whether at the beginning or end of your trip, a visit to the capital is crucial to understanding what makes this country tick. It is certainly worth spending some time here, and it can be an extremely rewarding destination after weeks spent in the countryside, offering fine restaurants, excellent museums, and all the comforts that a modern capital city has to offer. Guatemala City is also the country's transportation and business hub, so if you are trying to get around the country or are in Guatemala on business, you will find yourself on its streets sooner or later.

Most of the major attractions can be seen in a day or two. If you have more than two days to spend in Guatemala City, you might consider staying in Antigua to make better use of your time. Exceptions to this would be those in town for business looking for things to do after hours without taking a trip out of the city. Zona 10, conveniently near the airport, has some fine hotels and is home to a number of highly recommended museums. It is also one of the city's most attractive commercial and financial districts. A day strolling down pleasant Avenida La Reforma and sampling the Zona Viva's cafés, bars, nightclubs, and restaurants is a great way to cap off your visit to Guatemala.

ORIENTATION

Guatemala City's sprawl occupies about 400 square kilometers, filling a large valley scarred by deep ravines (known locally as *barrancos*) and surrounded by mountains and volcanoes. Its terrain gives the city a patchwork feel when viewed from the air, with parts of the city meandering fingerlike into the scarred landscape. The urban sprawl has also started migrating east and west into surrounding mountains. A large plateau atop the mountains abutting the city to the east is traversed by the Carretera a El Salvador (Road to El Salvador) and is one of the fastest-growing suburban sectors. The surrounding landscape is accentuated by the presence of active Pacaya Volcano, often visible at night, to the south. To the southwest, the cones of Agua, Fuego, and Acatenango Volcanoes can be seen rising above the mountain separating Guatemala City from neighboring Antigua Guatemala.

The city itself is divided into 25 zones, or *zonas*. Only a few of these hold any interest for the foreign visitor or resident. **Zonas 1 and 2** encompass the downtown sector, with **Zona 4** serving as a kind of transition zone between the original city core and newer business and residential sectors. **Zona 10** harbors the homes of wealthy elite, high-rise condominiums, hotels, restaurants, nightclubs, banks, and embassies. Moving south and abutting the airport, **Zona 14** is home to a large concentration of wealthy neighborhoods and high-rise condos. To the east and heading up the slopes of surrounding mountainsides lie residential **Zonas 15 and 16** and **Carretera a El Salvador.** Several of the city's *zonas* are separated from each other by natural boundaries, such as forested *barrancos*.

Unlike in Managua or San José, **street addresses** are very much in use here. Pay special attention when looking for street addresses, as the same street and house number can exist in more than one *zona*. Addresses usually begin with an avenue, or *avenida,* followed by a number with a dash. A typical street address would be something like: 7a Avenida 8-34 Zona 10. In this case, the "8" corresponds to the intersecting street number, or *calle*. The number after the dash is the house number. So the above address would be house number 34 between Eighth and Ninth Streets along 7th Avenue of Zona 10.

SAFETY

Guatemala City can be dodgy, though certain *zonas* are certainly safer than others. Most of the areas frequented by tourists are

the many contrasts of Guatemala City

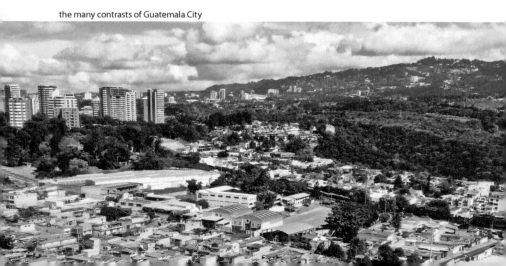

The Feel and Vibe of Guatemala City

Guatemala City might feel quite intimidating and downright scary. While crime, pollution, and noise cannot be denied, you've made it this far, so you should probably check things out for yourself and see it through your own eyes.

Guatemala City is Central America's largest city, with an approximate metro area population approaching four million inhabitants. The good news concerning the city's size is that you really have no reason to venture into more than about a third of its area. Much of the sprawl constituting the sizable metro area is found outside the official city limits and is composed of Guatemalan working-class subdivisions, industrial parks, and slums. The nicer parts of town are also conveniently located adjacent to each other, in the eastern third of the city near the airport. The downtown core lies to the north of the city's newer sectors.

Perhaps most fascinating about Guatemala City are the constant juxtapositions evidencing this vibrant capital's status as a microcosm of Guatemala's larger wealth and class disparities. Tin-roofed shacks cling to forested hillsides just out of view from the wooden decks of $500,000 homes. Buses trundle slowly down tree-lined boulevards while late-model BMWs zip by in the passing lane. Maya from the highlands dressed in traditional garb wait for these buses under steel-and-glass bus stop shelters advertising French perfumes.

Guatemala City feels more like a real city and not an overgrown town (sorry, San José), with actual buildings occupying a somewhat impressive portion of the urban sprawl. These buildings house condos, banks, hotels, and offices, giving the city a very modern feel. You'll see Guatemala's well-to-do frequenting the cafés, bars, restaurants, and hotels found in these sectors, along with travelers and foreign residents. Guatemalans love to be seen dining out in fine restaurants and shopping at exclusive stores for the latest fashions.

A darker side of Guatemala City's flashy displays of wealth is the shotgun-toting guards you'll find stationed outside of banks, gas stations, and fast-food franchises. The congregating of suit-wearing bodyguards outside gyms, restaurants, and private schools would be downright comical were it not such a flagrant reminder of the specter of extortionary kidnapping. And then there's the barbed wire—lots of it—and iron bars adorning many of the city's houses, which lie bunkered away in cordoned-off neighborhoods guarded by access gates staffed by security personnel. It all takes some getting used to, but we're fairly adaptable as a species.

Good or bad, love it or hate it, Guatemala City is what it is. If it all gets to be too much, just head up into the hills east of the city and look at it from above. It seems a lot more peaceful that way, framed by low-lying clouds and its gorgeous volcanic backdrop. Spend a few minutes picking out your favorite locations and seeing how many different parts of the city you can identify. It's a sight for sore eyes.

relatively safe, though the downtown area is considerably less safe than Zonas 10 and 14 and purse snatching and pickpocketing are serious problems. Exercise common sense and caution when in public areas. Riding public buses is not usually a good idea, though the newer Transmetro mass transit system has proven safer and is certainly more efficient. Transmetro buses are bright green and not to be confused with the Transurbano bus system (similar to the municipal buses).

Pay careful attention when using ATMs. Some thieves have been so ingenious as to set up keypads at the entrance to ATM kiosks asking cardholders to enter their PIN numbers in order to gain access to the machine. You should never enter your PIN number anywhere other than on the ATM keypad itself.

Watch out for another common scam, particularly in the vicinity of the airport, whereby a "Good Samaritan" informs you of a flat tire on your car. If that is indeed the case, pull over in a well-lighted, public place if you can but do not stop in the middle of the road to change the tire. He may try to carjack you. If you are able to make it to a public place such as a gas station, have someone in your party stay inside the car while another checks all four tires. If a tire is indeed flat, stay inside of or close to your car while someone changes the tire for you (it's common for gas station attendants to change tires in Guatemala). The important thing is not to lose sight of the inside of your vehicle for a moment. Thieves can be extremely crafty at distracting you and getting into your car while you take care of the urgent business at hand. Locked doors may be a deterrent but are not going to stop the thieves if they've targeted you. For information on other precautions and common scams to watch out for while traveling in Guatemala, see the State Department's Consular Information Sheet online at http://travel.state.gov.

Sights

Sights are listed by city zone, the official format for divvying up the city's land area. Most of the city's historic sites are found within the Centro Histórico. Some of the nicer museums are found near the airport in Zona 13 and in the Miraflores area west of the city center in Zona 11.

CENTRO HISTÓRICO

The original core of Guatemala City, dating to its foundation, is composed of 1a to 17 Calle and 1a to 12 Avenida, known today as the Centro Histórico. Most of the architecture is neoclassical, a sharp departure from the baroque architecture found in the previous capital of Antigua Guatemala. Few of the original buildings remain, having largely been destroyed by earthquakes in 1917 and 1976 or modified with the passing of time. Yet some excellent examples of the original architecture can still be found, and there is an ongoing campaign to restore several historic buildings in the downtown core. This program, known as RenaCENTRO, is a collaboration between several entities, including the local municipality, INGUAT, the private sector, and Argentinean, Spanish, and French cooperation.

Guatemala City was once nicknamed "The Silver Teacup" for its urban Spanish Renaissance design and architecture, including elegant theaters, large colonial mansions, broad avenues, imposing churches, and charming side streets. Although they have aesthetically deteriorated, they are not beyond rescue. This is precisely RenaCENTRO's mission: a multifaceted, holistic approach to restoring the grandeur of Guatemala's colonial-era capital. The restoration inexorably hinges upon local economic reactivation. Given Guatemala's huge tourism potential, it seems only fitting that its capital would become a welcome stop along the visitor's path, although restoration remains an ongoing process.

Parque Central

In typical Spanish colonial fashion, the city was laid out around a central plaza with a Catholic church and government buildings surrounding it. It is also known as the Plaza de la Constitución. The **Parque Central** encompasses a large area between 6a and 7a Avenidas and 6a and 8a Calles. Alongside it are the Palacio Nacional de la Cultura, Catedral Metropolitana, and Portal del Comercio. The park is usually abuzz with shoe shiners and folks enjoying a stroll through its grounds, now largely composed of concrete blocks with little greenery after being remodeled in the mid-1980s to include an underground parking lot. A large Guatemalan flag dominates the plaza near a small, sadly neglected monument to the 1996 peace accords; it consists of a glass case that once enclosed a flame, which has long since burned out. South of the park, heading towards 9a Calle is **Portal del Comercio,** a commercial arcade recently restored as part of RenaCENTRO's ongoing gentrification projects. Novena Calle (between 6a and 7a Avenidas) has also been restored as a pedestrian thoroughfare known as Pasaje Aycinena.

★ Palacio Nacional de la Cultura

Boston's Fenway Park has its Green Monster and so does Guatemala City. The former presidential palace, built between 1939 and 1943 during the time of maniacal dictator Jorge Ubico, is a large, green stone structure with elements of colonial and neoclassical architecture. The 1996 peace accords between the government and URNG guerrillas were signed here and the building was subsequently converted into a museum. It is also sometimes used to host visiting dignitaries such as former president George W. Bush and actor Mel Gibson. With most of Guatemala's presidents preferring to live in other parts of the city, it has not housed a president during a term in office since the early 1990s.

The Palacio Nacional de la Cultura (tel. 2239-5000, 9am-noon and 2pm-5pm daily, $5) is one of Guatemala City's most interesting attractions, as it affords the visitor a glimpse into Guatemala's colonial and dictatorial legacy. After all, Guatemala City was once the capital of the entire Central American isthmus and nowhere else in the region were colonial institutions so embedded in the national fiber. Similarly, Guatemala's *caudillos* (military strongmen) needed a residence befitting their status as rulers of a quasifeudal kingdom, to which end the palace served them quite well.

You can take a guided tour of the palace so as to better appreciate the intriguing architecture, including some Moorish courtyards, frescoed arches made of carved stone, and artwork by several Guatemalan artists of the 1940s. As you climb the wood-and-brass main stairway, you can admire a mural by Alredo Gálvez Suárez depicting a romanticized take on Guatemalan history. Stained-glass windows by Julio Urruela Vásquez and Roberto

González Goyri can be found adorning the palace in the second-floor banquet hall; they depict the virtues of good government. You might also be able to see the presidential balcony, which overlooks the plaza in classic dictatorial fashion.

A more modern-day attraction is the Patio de la Paz, where a stone sculpture of two hands commemorates the 1996 signing of the peace accords. A white rose held in the outstretched hands is changed at 11am by the palace guards once a week and on special occasions by visiting dignitaries. The rose used to be changed daily, but I guess it's one more thing we've lost to government cutbacks.

Catedral Metropolitana

The construction of Guatemala City's neoclassical Catedral Metropolitana (7a Avenida facing the plaza, 6am-noon and 2pm-7pm) began in 1782 and was completed in 1815, though the bell towers would not be completed until 1867. It has survived two earthquakes, a testament to its sturdy construction, even if it isn't exactly the prettiest of Guatemala's churches. The pillars on the church's facade are adorned with the names of many of Guatemala's disappeared, etched into the stone as a testament to the desire for justice, whether in this lifetime or the next. Inside, many of the altars and paintings adorning the church were brought here forcefully when the capital, along with its institutions, was officially moved to its current site from Antigua. The standout is the image of the Virgen del Perpetuo Socorro, Guatemala's oldest, brought into the country by Pedro de Alvarado in 1524.

Parque Centenario

Adjoining the larger central plaza, to the west, is the smaller Parque Centenario, with the Biblioteca Nacional (National Library) and Archivo General de Centroamérica (National Archive) bordering it. It occupies the former site of the Palacio Centenario, built to commemorate 100 years of independence from Spain. It briefly housed the National

Guatemala City (Zonas 1 and 4)

ZONA 3

ZONA 8

ZONA 1

ZONA 4

Santa Cecilia

To Amatitlán, Escuintla,
and Pacific Coast

28 CALLE
27 CALLE
26 CALLE
25 CALLE

24 CALLE
23 CALLE
22 CALLE
21 CALLE
20 CALLE
19 CALLE
18 CALLE
17 CALLE
16 CALLE
15 CALLE

1A AVENIDA
2A AVENIDA
3A AVENIDA
4A AVENIDA
5A AVENIDA
6A AVENIDA
7A AVENIDA
8A AVENIDA
10A AVENIDA
11 AVENIDA
12 AVENIDA
13 AVENIDA
16 AVENIDA

Bolívar

RUTA 8
VIA 1
RUTA 7
2 VIA 7
RUTA 6
RUTA 5
VIA 5
RUTA 4
VIA 4
RUTA 3
VIA 7
RUTA 2
RUTA 1
VIA 5

TRANSPORTES ALAMO
TRANSPORTES REBULI
TRANSPORTES VELÁSQUEZ
LINEAS AMERICA
VELOZ QUICHELENSE
TRANSPORTES TO CENTRA
TRANSPORTES GALGOS
TIPOGRAFIA NACIONAL
El Calvario
Plaza Barrios
FUENTES DEL NORTE
TRANSPORTES LOS HALCONES
TRANSPORTES ESCOBAR
MONJA BLANCA
TRANSPORTES FUENTES DEL POLOCHIC
LINEA DORADA
TRANSPORTES LITEGUA
RUTAS ORIENTALES
TRANSPORTES GUERRA
RAPIDOS DEL SUR

TEATRO AL AIRE LIBRE
Centro Cultural Miguel Angel Asturias
★ GRAN SALA
TEATRO DE CAMARA

FUENTE DE SAN JOSÉ
(MUSEO DEL EJÉRCITO)
MUNICIPALIDAD DE GUATEMALA
Centro Cívico
PUENTE DE LA PENITENCIARIA
DE LOS SUSPIROS
Cívico
Centro
Banco de Guatemala
INGUAT, OFICINA DE EXTRANJERIA

★ MUSEO DEL FERROCARRIL

Exposición
CONQUISTADOR HOTEL
4 Grados Sur
4 Grados Norte
4 GRADOS NORTE
TROVA JAZZ
Plaza de la República
TEATRO DEL INSTITUTO GUATEMALTECO AMERICANO

Estadio Nacional Mateo Flores

31 CALLE
30 CALLE
29 CALLE
28 CALLE
27 CALLE
26 CALLE
25 CALLE
24 CALLE
23 CALLE

Río Barranquilla

0   200 yds.
0   200 m

© AVALON TRAVEL

ZONA 3

AVENIDA ELENA

2A CALLE

AVENIDA ELENA

5A CALLE
6A CALLE
7A CALLE
4A CALLE
3A CALLE

1A AVENIDA

2A CALLE

1A AVENIDA A
1A AVENIDA A

1A CALLE

2A AVENIDA

11 CALLE
12 CALLE
13 CALLE
14 CALLE

10A CALLE

3A AVENIDA

CAFÉ DE IMERI ▼

3A AVENIDA

4A AVENIDA

2A AVENIDA

ARCHIVO GENERAL
DE CENTROAMERICA

5A AVENIDA

4A AVENIDA

SOMA CENTRO CULTURAL ■
LA BODEGUITA
DEL CENTRO ■

BIBLIOTECA
NACIONAL ★★

LAVANDERIA
EL SIGLO ■

HOTEL ●
PAN AMERICAN

PARQUE
CENTENARIO ★

LA CASA DE
CERVANTES ■

ARIN
CUAN ▼

5A AVENIDA

6A AVENIDA

RESTAURANTE
REY SOL ■

PALACIO NACIONAL
DE LA CULTURA ★

To Parque Minerva →

ALTUNA ▼
EUROPA BAR ▼

★ PORTAL DEL COMERCIO
LAS CIEN PUERTAS ★

EL
PORTAL

PARQUE
CENTRAL ★

CATEDRAL
METROPOLITANA ★

ZONA 2

6A AVENIDA

CENTRO CULTURAL
DE ESPAÑA ■
REILLY'S ▼
GUATE CITY ■

9A CALLE

LOS
CEBOLLINES ▼

CONGRESO DE
LA REPUBLICA ★

7A AVENIDA

8A AVENIDA

ZONA 1

7A AVENIDA

SAVOY ZONA UNO ▼

PASEO DE LA SEXTA

CENTRO
HISTÓRICO

9A AVENIDA

MERCADO
CENTRAL ★

LIN
CANOLA ■

8A AVENIDA

Parque
Concordia

IGLESIA DE
SAN FRANCISCO †
CUARTEL DE
★ POLICIA NACIONAL
HOTEL ●
COLONIAL

PALACIO DE CORREOS

10A AVENIDA

MUSEO NACIONAL
DE HISTORIA ★

10A AVENIDA

10A CALLE

10 AVENIDA A

1A CALLE

★ CASA MIMA

IGLESIA SAN MIGUEL
DE CAPUCHINAS †

11 AVENIDA

ZONA 1

8A CALLE

POSADA BELEN
MUSEUM INN ●

ZONA 1

TRANSPORTES
ZACULEU FUTURA ■

12 AVENIDA

7A CALLE

4A CALLE

EL CERRITO
DEL CARMEN †

IGLESIA SANTO
DOMINGO †

DIAGONAL 4

CALLE DE LAS TUNCHEZ

AVENIDA DE CANDELARIA

To Esquipulas,
Cobán, Quiriguá,
Livingston, and Copán

15 AVENIDA (AVENIDA DE LOS ARBOLES)

14 AVENIDA

15 AVENIDA

16 AVENIDA

5A CALLE

17 AVENIDA

Congress, whose building was burned to the ground in 1927. Its most interesting feature is a small acoustic shell amphitheater.

Mercado Central

Behind the cathedral is the city's **Mercado Central** (8a Avenida and 6a Calle, 6am-6pm Mon.-Sat., 9am-noon Sun.). The basement of the central market harbors produce, while the top two floors have a varied assortment of textiles, leather goods, and various handicrafts. It's a bit dark and bunkerlike, with the stalls packed to the ceiling with all kinds of goodies. It's also a bit overwhelming. The current market replaced the one destroyed by the 1976 earthquake. Be wary of pickpockets here.

Paseo de la Sexta

Historically, Sexta Avenida, otherwise known as "La Sexta," was the place to see and be seen. It was Guatemala City's most important thoroughfare, where the latest European fashions and luxury goods could be purchased from shops owned by Jewish, Spanish, and German immigrants. As the city expanded and its well-to-do moved south to Zonas 9, 10, and 13 during the 1970s, Sexta Avenida began a long, downward spiral.

As mentioned before, the downtown core of Guatemala City's historic Zona 1 has undergone urban renewal for some time now. In 2010 this process included the relocation of street vendors from the city's Sexta Avenida, at that time a disorganized mess choked by car traffic and sidewalks lined with those hawking everything from pirated DVDs to knock-off designer sunglasses. Today, the car traffic is gone and Sexta Avenida, along 10 blocks from the city's Plaza Central south to 18 Calle, has been renamed **Paseo de la Sexta.** An ongoing process, it has yielded remodeled art deco buildings, new lighting, sculptures, and a smattering of new cafés.

Although the area is much touted by the local media, don't expect to find a hip, trendy, and completely revamped downtown core. You also won't find cool streetside cafés or many good restaurants. This is Guatemala City, not Mexico City, and it's clear the wealthy prefer to stick to other parts of town. While you might expect to find new, slightly more upscale shops to line the newly upgraded streets of this pedestrian thoroughfare, the truth is the same shops continue to exist in slightly upgraded surroundings. If you're staying downtown, Paseo de la Sexta is worth a stop, but it's not yet a popular attraction with foreign travelers. Still, it provides

Paseo de la Sexta

a fascinating glimpse into the lives of working-class Guatemalan urbanites. Among the hubbub as you walk (or bike) down the thoroughfare, you'll find vendors curiously carrying full-sized and fully clothed mannequins on their backs or those selling ready-to-eat fruit and ceviche (only for the heartiest gringo stomachs). It's still not the safest part of town for a stroll, so be extra careful if you do venture out this way, as it's known for assorted riffraff, including pickpockets. There is a fair amount of police presence here, which is reassuring. The Transmetro now reaches this area, which makes it easier than ever to get to.

7a Avenida

Paralleling 6a Avenida is **7a Avenida,** with a variety of architectural highlights. Among these is the splendid **Palacio de Correos** (Central Post Office, 8:30am-5pm Mon.-Fri., 8:30am-1pm Sat.), at the corner of 7a Avenida and 12 Calle, featuring a large archway that reaches over to the building across the street. Also attractive is the nearby **Tipografía Nacional** (National Printing Press), at the corner of 7a Avenida and 18 Calle. It dates to 1894 and somewhat resembles a gingerbread house.

Both 6a and 7a Avenidas continue their straight course southward through Zonas 4 and 9 before ending at a series of archways marking the northern extreme of the airport runway.

Museums

One block east of the market and one block south on 10a Avenida is the **Museo Nacional de Historia** (9a Calle 9-70 Zona 1, tel. 2253-6149, museonh@hotmail.com, 9am-4:30pm Mon.-Fri., $1.50) with historical documents, clothing, and paintings, largely to do with Guatemala's tyrannical rulers. Among the more interesting exhibits are some photographs by Eadweard Muybridge, who visited and photographed the country in 1875. The museum is housed in a very attractive colonial building.

Casa Mima (8a Avenida 14-12 Zona 1, tel. 2253-6657, www.casamima.org, 10am-5pm Mon.-Sat., $3) offers a fascinating peek into the lives of Guatemala's upper middle class from generations past. The splendidly restored 19th-century town house is furnished in art deco, Victorian, and French neo-rococo styles. Guided tours are available and must be arranged one week in advance. **La Casa de Cervantes** (5a Calle 5-18 Zona 1, tel. 2251-8120, http://casadecervantes.com,

a detail from La Casa de Cervantes

free) showcases fair trade goods in Guatemala and has a gift shop, where you can purchase fair trade coffee, handicrafts, and even locally made kombucha. There's a small café with pleasant outdoor seating in an old courtyard and a bookstore packed with excellent titles documenting subjects of Guatemalan history and social justice. There are periodic exhibitions and special events. It's more of an information and cultural center than a museum but is certainly worth a look. It was being repainted with artwork from a local muralist during my last visit.

Train enthusiasts will enjoy **Museo del Ferrocarril** (in front of the intersection of 9a Avenida and 20 Calle, tel. 2232-9270, www. museofegua.com, 9am-4pm Tues.-Fri., 10am-4pm Sat.-Sun., $0.25), housed in a refurbished building that was once the city's train station. The state-run railways, known then as FEGUA, were privatized during the Arzú administration. Among the attractions are several steam engines, train cars, and exhibits of train paraphernalia, including some wonderful old photographs. Some cool classic cars are also on display here.

The **Centro Cultural de España** (6a Avenida 11-02 Zona 1, Edificio Lux, Nivel 2, tel. 2503-7500, www.cceguatemala.org, 10am-7pm Tues.-Fri., 10am-2pm Sat., free) shows movies most nights, hosts workshops and art exhibits, and has a small library. It makes a nice addition to the city's Paseo de la Sexta, having moved here from its old location at the now defunct 4 Grados Norte.

Churches

Several of the city's downtown churches have been restored in recent years and might be worth a stop to admire their noteworthy architecture. Construction on **Iglesia de San Francisco** (6a Avenida and 13 Calle Zona 1, 7am-noon and 2pm-7pm daily) began in 1800 and wasn't completed until 1851. Its charming light gray exterior has been worn down by the elements; inside are 18 altars of impressive quality. Another beautiful church is that of **Iglesia Santo Domingo** (12 Avenida and 10a Calle), constructed between 1792 and 1808. In addition to its attractive architecture, it is known for its paintings, including one depicting the apparition of the Virgin Mary to Santo Domingo de Guzmán, after whom the capital of the Dominican Republic is named. (It is believed he received the rosary from her.) **El Cerrito del Carmen** (12 Avenida and 2a Calle Zona 1, 7am-noon and 2pm-6pm daily) denominates both the name of this hermitage and the hill on which it rests, with wonderful views of the downtown area. It dates to 1620 and is known for its image of a virgin of the same name embossed in silver, a gift from Carmelite nuns in the 17th century. Oil paintings by Tomás de Merlo adorn the inside of **Iglesia San Miguel de Capuchinas** (10 Avenida 10-51 Zona 1, 6am-noon and 2pm-7pm daily), with its transitional baroque-neoclassical architecture.

ZONA 2
Parque Minerva

As you head north along 6a Avenida and then Avenida Simeón Cañas, it's about 1.5 kilometers from the city center to Parque Minerva in the adjoining Zona 2 sector. The park here has some sporting facilities, including the **Estadio de Béisbol Enrique "Trapo" Torrebiarte,** where there are sometimes games on weekends. Its informal atmosphere is a bit like that of old-time minor league parks in the U.S. Midwest. Baseball is nowhere near as popular in Guatemala as in other parts of Central America, namely Nicaragua, but if you're a fan of the game, you might want to stop and check it out.

The park's main attraction, however, is also one of Guatemala's most unusual. The 2,000-square-meter **Mapa en Relieve** (Relief Map, Ave. Simeón Cañas Final, Hipódromo Del Norte, Zona 2, tel. 5632-5708, www.mapaenrelieve.org, 9am-5pm daily, $0.75) is built to 1:10,000 scale and was created in 1905, well before the invention of Google Earth. It gives you a good idea of the country's mountain topography and the contrasting flatness of Petén and neighboring Belize, which, of course, is included as part of Guatemala in accord with the long-standing border dispute. The scale of the mountains is somewhat exaggerated, with the volcanoes and peaks looking steep and pointy. There are observation towers from which you can get a better vantage point. The rivers and lakes are sometimes filled with water from built-in taps, making for an even more authentic experience. It makes a good stop if you're in Guatemala City before heading out to the interior and want to get a feel for the country's unique geography.

Museo de los Mártires

A fascinating glimpse into Guatemala's tragic (and largely unknown) history can be found in Zona 2's **Museo de los Mártires del Movimiento Sindical, Estudiantil y Popular de Guatemala** (1a. Calle 1-53 Zona 2, tel. 2232-4853, www.fafg.org, donations accepted). Forensic anthropology has come a long way in recent years in helping to identify the victims of Guatemala's 45,000 cases of forced disappearance during the civil war. The museum stands as a testament to the lives of almost 200 victims based on information found in a military archive detailing date of disappearance and death. There's a video presentation, clothing and personal items left behind by the victims, and a tribute to forensic anthropologists in their search for the truth. The victims' mug shots and file information are chillingly reproduced on a wall, giving a face and voice to the victims of Guatemala's dirty war.

ZONA 4

A revitalization program gave Zona 4 a distinct character in recent years with the establishment of a pedestrian thoroughfare known as 4 Grados Norte, lined with sidewalk cafés and restaurants during the day, doubling as bars at night. While it was a good idea in theory, it soon attracted a motley assortment of drug dealers and local riffraff. The restaurants and bars have mostly closed their doors, but the area is enjoying a renaissance as a center for technology-based businesses. The *New York Times* compared it to Silicon Valley in a 2011 story featuring the area's Campus Tec building. Dozens of new technology start-ups have sprung up here in recent years. Some of the postproduction for Hollywood movies now takes place here, including that for *The Chronicles of Narnia*.

Further adding luster to this area is the appearance of food trucks in a space fronting the pleasant **Plaza de La República** (7a

The disappeared from Guatemala's civil war are remembered at Zona 2's Museo de los Mártires.

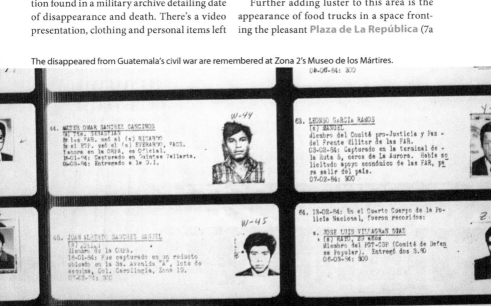

Avenida y Ruta 5). The food trucks serving Chinese food, burgers, and tacos are a popular lunchtime option with workers in nearby office towers.

Zona 4's other main attraction is a dilapidated bus terminal for second-class buses, though this was expected to fall into disuse with the municipal government's plans to move all bus traffic out of the city.

Centro Cívico

As you head south from the downtown sectors of Zonas 1 and 2, you'll come to a transitional area between the old city core and some of the newer parts of town. Some guidebooks refer to the latter as the "new city," which to the best of my knowledge has never been used by locals to describe their city layout. As the city spread south from the central area, urban planners and architects decided to build around a concept of a civic center to house some of the more important government buildings. Thus was born the **Centro Cívico.** Today it houses Guatemala's **Corte Suprema de Justicia** (Supreme Court), **Banco de Guatemala** (Bank of Guatemala), **Municipalidad de Guatemala** (City Hall), and the administrative offices of the

Guatemala Tourist Commission (7a Avenida 1-17 Zona 4, 8am-4pm Mon.-Fri.). There's the occasional exhibit in the lobby and you can get some tourist information, including maps, but you're probably better off picking these up at the information kiosks at the international airport.

Centro Cultural Miguel Ángel Asturias

Inaugurated in 1968 and named after Guatemala's Nobel Prize-winning author, the capital's national theater is built on a hill once harboring the fort of San José de Buena Vista, destroyed by artillery fire during the October Revolution of 1944. The **Centro Cultural Miguel Ángel Asturias** (mcd.gob.gt/teatronacional) consists of a **Gran Sala** (Great Theater) with a seating capacity of 2,041, an outdoor amphitheater seating 2,500, the 320-seat **Teatro de Cámara** (Chamber Theater), and several smaller venues. It has some interesting architecture designed by Efrín Recinos, and its hilltop location overlooking the rest of the civic center gives it an air of grandeur. The center still hosts frequent events, including ballet and theater productions. Check local listings for more information.

Zona 4's Centro Cívico

ZONA 7
Parque Arqueológico Kaminaljuyú

This Mayan site occupied the valley where Guatemala City now stands. It was first settled sometime around 400 BC and grew to house an abundance of flat-topped pyramids (with the remains of nobility buried underneath) by AD 100. The first inhabitants of the site appear to have been some early cultures (Las Charcas, Miraflores, and Esperanza, dating from 1500 BC to AD 150), which established a foundation for the later development of the Classic Mayan culture here. These early cultures are characterized by the development of agriculture, weaving, pottery making, and ritual burial of the dead in temple mounds and shrines. Central to the city's rapid population growth was the construction of a series of irrigation canals drawing upon the ancient lake of Miraflores. Eventually the lake began to dry out, leading to widespread migration out of the city. Its Chol-speaking inhabitants are thought to have moved on to El Salvador and maybe even Copán, Honduras. The site's historical record fades out (momentarily) sometime between the 2nd and 3rd centuries AD.

With the rise of Central Mexico's Teotihuacán in the 5th century, the Guatemalan highlands received a large influx of invaders from the north. Here the invaders established their regional capital, constructing new temples and structures, and flourished with the control of trade networks around highly prized obsidian and jade. It is thought that, along with its powerful neighbor to the north, Kaminaljuyú exercised considerable influence over the Petén lowland sites, in particular Tikal. One of Tikal's rulers, Curl Nose, may actually have come from here in AD 387.

The site was first excavated in 1925 and yielded potsherds and clay figurines from the early cultures. Its larger extent and importance were discovered in 1935 when a local football team uncovered a buried structure after cutting away the edges of two inconspicuous mounds to lengthen their practice field. Today the site is really no more than a series of mounds. Though the site is in Zona 7 proper, the best place to see it is actually near the Museo Miraflores in adjacent Zona 11, where you can tour the excellent museum and see some temple mounds.

ZONA 9

Part of the city's newer sector, Zona 9 adjoins Zona 4 and is crossed by 6a and 7a Avenidas. Along 7a Avenida, on 2a Calle, is an Eiffel Tower-like monument commemorating the rule of Guatemala's liberal reformer Justo Rufino Barrios (1871-1885), known as **Torre del Reformador.** Wonderfully illuminated at night with a large spinning spotlight at its top, the steel tower serves as a nice backdrop for an annual December fireworks show. A bell at top is rung every year on June 30 in remembrance of the Liberal victory in the revolution of 1871. It was a project of the Ubico administration and was not a donation from France, as is commonly thought. The bell tower, however, was a gift from Belgium. Nearby, at the corner of 5a Calle and Avenida La Reforma is **Plaza Estado de Israel,** honoring the creation of the Jewish state with a giant Star of David sculpture.

Also along Avenida La Reforma, between 2a Calle and Calle Mariscal Cruz, is the **Jardín Botánico y Museo de Historia Natural** (Botanical Gardens and Natural History Museum, tel. 2334-6064, 8am-3pm Mon.-Fri., 9am-noon Sat., $1.50), managed by the Universidad de San Carlos. It's really only recommendable for the botanical gardens, which offer a nice respite from the chaotic traffic just beyond its walls. The plant species are all labeled in Spanish and Latin. Give the natural history museum a skip unless you're really into bad taxidermy.

At 7a Avenida and 12 Calle is the **Plazuela España,** a circular miniplaza circumvented by traffic and featuring a pretty fountain built in honor of Spain's King Carlos III in 1789. It originally was in the city's central park, where it had a large equestrian statue that disappeared shortly after independence from

Guatemala City (Zonas 9, 10, 13, and 14)

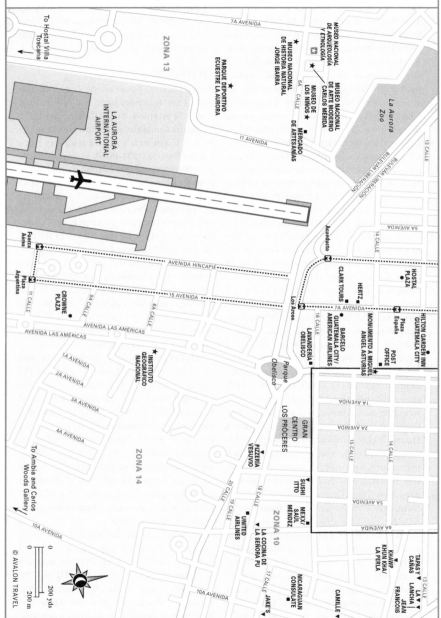

ZONA 13

To Hostal Villa Toscana

7A AVENIDA

MUSEO NACIONAL DE ARQUEOLOGÍA Y ETNOLOGÍA

MUSEO NACIONAL DE HISTORIA NATURAL JORGE IBARRA

PARQUE DEPORTIVO ECUESTRE LA AURORA

MUSEO DE LOS NIÑOS

6A CALLE

MUSEO NACIONAL DE ARTE MODERNO CARLOS MERIDA

MERCADO DE ARTESANÍAS

11 AVENIDA

La Aurora Zoo

BULEVAR LIBERACIÓN

13 CALLE

LA AURORA INTERNATIONAL AIRPORT

Acueducto

14 CALLE

5A AVENIDA

Fuerza Aérea

Plaza Argentina

11 CALLE

AVENIDA HINCAPIÉ

CLARK TOURS

HOSTAL PLAZA

CROWNE PLAZA

9A CALLE

15 AVENIDA

6A CALLE

Los Arcos

HERTZ

7A AVENIDA

16 CALLE

Plaza España

HILTON GARDEN INN GUATEMALA CITY

AVENIDA LAS AMÉRICAS

AVENIDA LAS AMÉRICAS

INSTITUTO GEOGRÁFICO NACIONAL

1A AVENIDA

2A AVENIDA

3A AVENIDA

4A AVENIDA

ZONA 14

To Ambia and Carlos Woods Gallery

10A AVENIDA

LAVANDERÍA OBELISCO

BARCELO GUATEMALA CITY/ AMERICAN AIRLINES

MONUMENTO A MIGUEL ÁNGEL ASTURIAS

POST OFFICE

Parque Obelisco

GRAN CENTRO LOS PRÓCERES

PIZZERIA VESUVIO

20 CALLE

19 CALLE

18 CALLE

SUSHI ITTO

MEXXI/ SAÚL MENDEZ

UNITED AIRLINES

LA COCINA DE LA SEÑORA PU

ZONA 10

10A AVENIDA

1A AVENIDA

2A AVENIDA

15 CALLE

14 CALLE

5A AVENIDA

6A AVENIDA

13 CALLE

TAPAS Y CAÑAS

KHAWP KHUN KHA/ LA PERLA

NICARAGUAN CONSULATE

CAMILLE

17 CALLE

JAKE'S

LA PERLA

LANCHA

JEAN FRANCOIS

© AVALON TRAVEL

0   200 yds
0   200 m

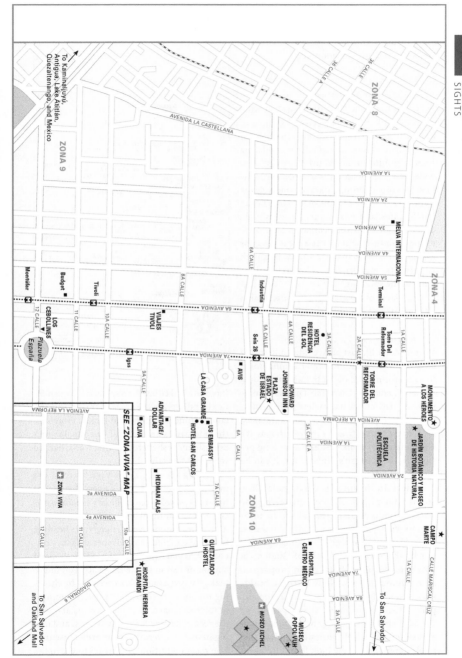

To Kaminaljuyú,
Antigua, Lake Atitlán,
Quezaltenango, and Mexico

ZONA 9

ZONA 8

36 CALLE A

36 CALLE

AVENIDA LA CASTELLANA

1A AVENIDA

2A AVENIDA

3A AVENIDA

4A AVENIDA

5A AVENIDA

MELVA INTERNACIONAL

ZONA 4

6A CALLE

Terminal

Torre Del
Reformador

1A CALLE

2A CALLE

8A CALLE

4A CALLE

HOTEL
RESIDENCIA
DEL SOL

3A CALLE

TORRE DEL
REFORMADOR

Montúfar

Budget

Tivoli

LOS
CEBOLLINES

12 CALLE

11 CALLE

10A CALLE

VIAJES
TIVOLI

Plazuela
España

Igss

9A CALLE

Industri

Seis 26

5A CALLE

6A AVENIDA

7A AVENIDA

AVIS

LA CASA GRANDE

PLAZA
ESTADO
DE ISRAEL

HOWARD
JOHNSON INN

MONUMENTO
A LOS HÉROES

JARDÍN BOTÁNICO Y MUSEO
DE HISTORIA NATURAL

AVENIDA LA REFORMA

AVENIDA LA REFORMA

CAMPO
MARTE

CALLE MARISCAL CRUZ

1A CALLE

SEE "ZONA VIVA" MAP

ADVANTAGE/
DOLLAR

OLIVA

US EMBASSY

HOTEL SAN CARLOS

6A
CALLE

ESCUELA
POLITÉCNICA

3A CALLE A

1A AVENIDA

2A AVENIDA

ZONA VIVA

3a AVENIDA

4a AVENIDA

HEDMAN ALAS

7A CALLE

ZONA 10

6A AVENIDA

QUETZALROO
HOSTEL

HOSPITAL
CENTRO MÉDICO

7A AVENIDA

8A AVENIDA

1A CALLE

3A CALLE

To San Salvador

12 CALLE

11 CALLE

10a
CALLE

HOSPITAL HERRERA
LLERANDI

DIAGONAL 6

To San Salvador
and Oakland Mall

MUSEO IXCHEL

MUSEO
POPOL VUH

Spain. Its current location was a move by the Ubico administration. Some once-attractive but now deteriorated tile benches are on the sidewalks opposite the fountain.

ZONA 10
Avenida La Reforma

Running between 1a Calle and 20 Calle, Avenida La Reforma is a classic example of the 19th-century trend, common throughout Latin America's major capitals, of emulating French architectural and urban design with wide, tree-lined boulevards adorned with statues. This broad thoroughfare separates Zonas 9 and 10 and features some of the city's better hotels, cafés, and restaurants along its path. The wide, grassy median contains some interesting sculptures and makes a great place for a stroll or bike ride thanks to a new bike path running its entire length. La Reforma culminates at the spacious **Parque Obelisco,** featuring a large obelisk, a gigantic Guatemalan flag, palm trees, a fountain, and sitting areas.

★ Zona Viva

Within Zona 10, east of Avenida La Reforma all the way to 6a Avenida and running north to south from 10a Calle to 16 Calle, the **Zona Viva** is Guatemala City's most pleasant commercial district, with a variety of hip cafés, trendy boutiques, lively bars and nightclubs, excellent restaurants, and expensive hotels. It's Guatemala City at its best and after long periods in the country's hinterlands, it can be downright refreshing.

Unlike in downtown Guatemala City, you'll find plenty of trees sheltering the streets from the harsh tropical sun in addition to wide, pedestrian-friendly sidewalks. Zona Viva's many high-rise buildings harbor banks, offices, the bulk of Guatemala City's international hotel chain properties, and condominiums. None of these buildings is more than 20 stories high, as the airport's proximity limits vertical expansion of the adjacent areas, giving the neighborhood a cosmopolitan feel without the claustrophobic concrete-jungle look found in larger

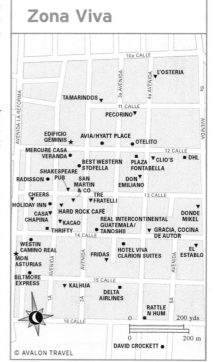

Zona Viva

© AVALON TRAVEL

international cities. Interspersed between office buildings are the area's many dining and entertainment options and tucked away into the side streets are some of Guatemala's nicest residences sheltered behind walls, barbed wire, and bougainvillea.

During the day, Zona Viva's streets are mostly the haunt of businesspeople because of the area's prominence as the city's main financial district. By night, especially on weekends, it becomes the enclave of young folks heading to bars and nightclubs or dinner at a fancy restaurant. If you find yourself needing to spend a night or two in Guatemala City, you might make it a very enjoyable experience by checking into one of the area's attractive boutique or international chain hotels, eating at one of the recommended local restaurants, and taking in one or several of the nearby museums. The recent addition of a hostel to the area's accommodations means this is no longer just an option for wealthy travelers. It is also conveniently close to the airport.

★ Museo Ixchel

The city's most magnificent museum, Museum Ixchel (6a Calle Final Zona 10, tel. 2361-8081/2, www.museoixchel.org, 9am-5pm Mon.-Fri., 9am-1pm Sat., $4 adults, $2 students, $15-80 for guided tours in English) on the grounds of the Francisco Marroquín University, is dedicated to Mayan culture with an emphasis on weaving and traditional costumes. It's housed in a beautiful brick building built to resemble a Mayan *huipil,* or handwoven, embroidered blouse. On display are pre-Hispanic objects, photographs, handwoven fabrics, ceremonial costumes, weaving tools, and folk paintings by Guatemalan artist Andrés Curruchich. You'll find interactive multimedia displays, a café, bookstore, and *huipiles* for sale in the excellent gift shop. Displays are in English and Spanish. This museum is a must-see for anyone with even a casual interest in Mayan weaving, as it manages to condense the country's rich weaving heritage spanning a fairly vast geographical range into a single place with excellent displays and an attractive setting.

Museo Popol Vuh

Next door and also on the university campus is the similarly high-caliber Museo Popol Vuh (tel. 2361-2301, www.popolvuh.ufm.edu, 9am-5pm Mon.-Fri., 9am-1pm Sat., $4 adults, $2 students). Started in 1978 with a university donation by private collectors, it has been in its current location since 1997. The museum houses an impressive collection from Guatemala's archaeological record grouped in different rooms denoted by Preclassic, Classic, Postclassic, and Colonial themes. The highlight is in the Postclassic room with a replica of the *Dresden Codex,* one of only three Mayan books to survive their postconquest burning by the Spanish (the other two are the *Paris Codex* and the *Madrid Codex*).

ZONA 11
★ Museo Miraflores

The excellent Museo Miraflores (7a Calle 21-55 Zona 11, Paseo Miraflores, tel. 2470-3415, 9am-7pm Tues., Wed., Sun., 9am-8pm Thurs., Fri., Sat., $5 adults, $1 children and students) is dedicated to the history of the Mayan site of Kaminaljuyú. Just outside the museum's main entrance is a replica of an irrigation canal similar to those found throughout the Mayan city as early as 600 BC. Inside,

a statue of Nobel Prize laureate Miguel Ángel Asturias on Avenida La Reforma

the large window panels provide fantastic views of the stark contrast between old and new, with the green temple mound of structure B-V-3 flanked by modern glass buildings in the background. Also at the entrance is a scale model of what the city probably looked like in its heyday, built into the museum floor under a glass case. In the main exhibit area, you'll find a comprehensive history of Kaminaljuyú in English and Spanish as well as a burial display, pottery, jade jewelry, stone sculpture, and obsidian blades. There are also old photographs of the site's excavation and maps showing the large area once occupied by the ancient city. You are free to explore the temple mounds outside (steps are built into them). A few more temple mounds can be found in the vicinity of the museum, having been completely closed in by one of the city's larger shopping complexes. Among the latter are the ever-growing Galerías Miraflores, Paseo Miraflores, and Las Majadas.

ZONA 13

This area was once the site of a large farm known as La Aurora, which today gives its name to the zoo, airport, and adjacent horse track on the grounds of the former Hipódromo del Sur. The horse track has been reinvented as Parque Deportivo Ecuestre La Aurora.

Zona 13 also houses a number of fairly good museums, all adjacent to each other in a large complex, and the city's zoo.

La Aurora Zoo

Guatemala City's La Aurora Zoo (Boulevard Juan Pablo II Zona 13, tel. 2475-0894, http://aurorazoo.org.gt, 9am-5pm Tues.-Sun., $4 adults, $1.50 children) is modern and well run. Its grounds are a popular weekend destination for city dwellers from all walks of life. About 900 animals representing 110 species are housed in re-creations of their natural habitats, including African savannah, Asia, and tropical forest. There are leopards, lions, giraffes, Asian pachyderms, Bengal tigers, and jaguars and other species found in

Guatemala's tropical forests. All cages have been removed from the park so as to provide visitors with the opportunity to see the animals free of visual obstructions. Check out the English teahouse dating to 1924. Penguins were the most recent addition to the zoo at last visit. Three Bengal tiger cubs were born and introduced to the public here in 2014, to the delight of spectators. They will likely find residency in a North American or European zoo by the time you read this, in an effort to maintain the gene pool of this highly endangered species.

Museo de los Niños

Right across the street is the Museo de los Niños (Children's Museum, 5a Calle 10-00 Zona 13, tel. 2475-5076, www.museodelosninos.com.gt, 8:30am-noon and 1pm-4:30pm Tues.-Fri., 9:30am-1:30pm and 2:30pm-6pm Sat.-Sun. and holidays, $5), housed in a pyramidal building, with educational exhibits and hands-on learning on themes such as civic values and teamwork. You'll also find a giant jigsaw puzzle of Guatemala, a music room, and trampolines. It's a popular school field trip.

★ Museo Nacional de Arqueología y Etnología

The city's Museo Nacional de Arqueología y Etnología (6a Calle y 7a Avenida Zona 13, tel. 2475-4399, www.munae.gob.gt, 9am-4pm Tues.-Fri., 9am-noon and 1:30pm-4pm Sat.-Sun., $7.50) houses an outstanding collection of original monuments from Guatemala's archaeological sites, including ceramics, carved rock sculptures and stelae from Kaminaljuyú, barrigones (Olmecoid stone figures with distended, bloated bellies) from the Pacific Coast sites, and stelae from the Petén sites. Among the latter are beautifully carved stelae and a spectacular hieroglyphic bench from Piedras Negras as well as stelae and hieroglyphic panels from Dos Pilas and Machaquilá. Another of the archaeology and ethnologgy museum's highlights is a splendid jade mask made famous on the cover of the September 1987 issue

a Maya stela on display in the Museo Nacional de Arqueología y Etnología

Rodolfo Abularach, reminiscent of Picasso's *Guernica.*

Museo Nacional de Historia Natural Jorge Ibarra

For all of Guatemala's rich ecology, it still lacks a comprehensive natural history museum to do it justice. The **Museo Nacional de Historia Natural Jorge Ibarra** (6a Calle 7-30 Zona 13, tel. 2472-0468, 9am-4pm Tues.-Fri., 9am-noon and 2pm-4pm Sat.-Sun., $1.50) makes an attempt but falls short. You'll find plenty of taxidermy as well as exhibits on several of the country's ecosystems. A standout is the photo exhibit on the Atitlán pied-billed grebe, extinct since 1987, and the attempt in the mid-20th century to save it.

ZONA 14

Guatemala City's boom district, Zona 14 has grown by leaps and bounds in recent years thanks to a plethora of new condos and office buildings built in this area. The sector's main feature is **Avenida Las Américas,** which is really just a continuation of Zona 9/10's Avenida La Reforma and boasts the same sylvan landscaping interspersed with monuments to Columbus and other historical figures centered around wide plazas. At the end of this avenue is a steep drop-off and Plaza Berlin, from which there are good views of the city's southern sprawl and Pacaya Volcano, along with some simple snack and drink stands. An addition to this plaza are three pieces of none other than the now-departed Berlin Wall, with a plaque commemorating liberty.

Avenida Las Américas parallels La Aurora Airport's runway. Branching off from the main artery are a number of side streets and residential areas. Two-story houses now share these streets with 20- and 30-story commercial and residential buildings. Between the airport runway and Avenida Las Américas is Avenida Hincapié, where the hangars of some of the domestic carriers and helicopter flights are housed just off its juncture with 18 Calle.

On Sundays, a stretch from Avenida Las

of *National Geographic.* The ethnology section has displays on traditional costumes and housing. The exhibits are not quite as modern or well executed as those in some other of the city's top museums, but the sheer significance of the original pieces found here makes a visit more than worthwhile.

Museo Nacional de Arte Moderno Carlos Mérida

Across the street is the city's **Museo Nacional de Arte Moderno Carlos Mérida** (tel. 2472-0467, 9am-4pm Tues.-Fri., 9am-noon and 1:30pm-4pm Sat.-Sun., $2.50), which focuses largely on the work of its namesake artist, including examples of his Cubist art and large murals. Mérida's Guatemala's most celebrated artist; his work also adorns the inside of several buildings in Guatemala City's Civic Center, including City Hall, with a giant mural known as *Canto a la Raza* (*Ode to the Race*), recently restored. Among the other interesting works found at the museum of modern art is one titled *La Peste* (*Pestilence*) by

Zonas 15, 16, and Carretera a El Salvador

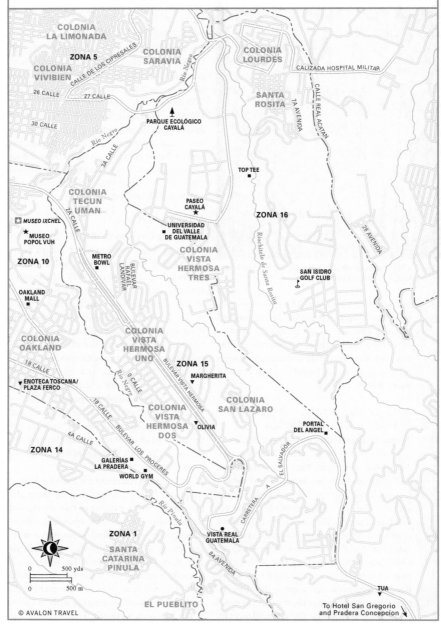

COLONIA
LA LIMONADA

ZONA 5

COLONIA
SARAVIA

COLONIA
LOURDES

CALIZADA HOSPITAL MILITAR

COLONIA
VIVIBIEN

CALLE DE LOS CIPRESALES

26 CALLE   27 CALLE

SANTA
ROSITA

CALLE REAL ACATAN

7A AVENIDA

30 CALLE

Río Negro

PARQUE ECOLÓGICO
CAYALÁ

3A CALLE

TOP TEE ■

COLONIA
TECUN
UMAN

PASEO
CAYALÁ ★

ZONA 16

26 AVENIDA

2A CALLE

☒ MUSEO IXCHEL

★ MUSEO
POPOL VUH

UNIVERSIDAD
DEL VALLE
DE GUATEMALA

Riachuelo de Santa Rosita

ZONA 10

METRO
BOWL ■

COLONIA
VISTA
HERMOSA
TRES

SAN ISIDRO
GOLF CLUB

BULEVAR
RAFAEL
LANDIVAR

OAKLAND
MALL ■

COLONIA
OAKLAND

COLONIA
VISTA
HERMOSA
UNO

ZONA 15

18 CALLE

Río Negro

0 CALLE

BULEVAR VISTA HERMOSA

MARGHERITA ▼

▼ ENOTECA TOSCANA/
PLAZA FERCO

COLONIA
SAN LAZARO

18 CALLE   BULEVAR LOS PROCERES

COLONIA
VISTA
HERMOSA
DOS

OLIVIA ▼

PORTAL
DEL ANGEL ■

4A CALLE

EL SALVADOR

ZONA 14

GALERÍAS ■
LA PRADERA ■
WORLD GYM

CARRETERA A

Río Pinula

ZONA 1

SANTA
CATARINA
PINULA

VISTA REAL ■
GUATEMALA

8A AVENIDA

0   500 yds

0   500 m

TUA ▼

EL PUEBLITO

To Hotel San Gregorio
and Pradera Concepcion ▶

© AVALON TRAVEL

Américas all the way to Avenida La Reforma's Plaza Israel is closed to pedestrian traffic, making for a very pleasant place to take a stroll.

ZONAS 15 AND 16

Also enjoying substantial growth due to new condos and office buildings are Zonas 15 and 16, on the eastern edge of Guatemala City bordering ravines and the hillside leading up to a neighboring plateau. In addition to the area's prominence as an affluent residential sector, it also houses joint retail/residential centers such as the ever-expanding Paseo Cayalá with condos, an outdoor shopping mall, gym, and even a driving range. It's pleasantly urbanized while feeling like you're well outside of the city core, seen off in the distance separated by deep gorges. Among the main thoroughfares is Bulevar Vista Hermosa, leading southeast out of the city.

Carretera a El Salvador

From Bulevar Vista Hermosa, the road winds out of the city and up a mountainside heading southeast, eventually making its way to neighboring El Salvador. The first 35 kilometers or so of this Carretera a El Salvador are Guatemala City's suburb extraordinaire.

After climbing up the mountains to the east of Guatemala City, the road eventually traverses a plateau, providing the perfect topographic conditions for the establishment of a virtual satellite city. The area around Carretera a El Salvador is also prime agricultural land. You'll find countless subdivisions springing up all over this fast-growing area, giving it all the feel of a U.S. suburb. The plateau lies at an altitude of about 2,135 meters (7,000 feet), so it's a bit cooler than Guatemala City and it also receives more rainfall during the rainy season. Those familiar with San José, Costa Rica, might find this area very similar to the Escazú suburbs near that city.

Although it's very much a residential area, you may find yourself visiting friends or staying at one of the hotels in this neck of the woods. Catering to the ever-increasing numbers of Guatemala City residents migrating to the surrounding suburbs, the area has at least one sizable shopping mall in Pradera Concepción, which adjoins the Condado Concepción shopping district. Between them, they boast a number of restaurants, PriceSmart warehouse shopping, WalMart, Sears, banks, car dealerships, a Starbucks, and even an IMAX movie theater. The selection of goods in local supermarkets

aerial view of Guatemala City's Zona 10 looking east to Zonas 15 and 16

is more upscale (with prices to match), so a lot of folks looking for favorite import items do their shopping up here. This area is also home to two of Guatemala's most upscale golf courses and one of the city's finest hotels. Also in this area, and once used as a little-known shortcut for getting out of the city, Muxbal has recently seen the rise of upscale shopping centers housing some of my favorite eateries.

Entertainment

NIGHTLIFE

Guatemala City has a fairly lively nightlife scene with bars, clubs, and music found mostly in the Zona Viva and downtown. There are plenty of places to dance to salsa and Latin beats in addition to rock and pop music. Electronica is also a big hit with Guatemalan partygoers. DJ Tiësto performs in Guatemala fairly frequently.

Bars

A good mix of bars in the downtown area caters to the city's bohemian population as well as to international travelers. In Zona 10, the Zona Viva sector centered around 16 Calle is the place to go if you want to hang out with the city's wealthy elite in the hippest establishments.

Downtown, El Portal (Portal del Comercio, 9a Calle, between 6a and 7a Avenidas, 10am-10pm Mon.-Sat.) is said to be the old stomping grounds of none other than Che Guevara, who lived in Guatemala City in the early 1950s. You'll find a long wooden bar and some wooden tables along with draft beers for about $2. The entrance is at the Portal del Comercio arcade ingress on the south side of the park along 6a Avenida. Nearby Las Cien Puertas (9a Calle between 6a and 7a Avenidas, Pasaje Aycinena, Zona 1, tel. 2232-8502, noon-2am Mon.-Sat.) is the city's quintessential bohemian hangout set in a restored colonial arcade. Enjoy tasty quesadillas and tacos when you get the munchies. Europa Bar (11 Calle 5-16, Edificio Testa, Local 201, tel. 2253-4929, 8am-midnight Mon.-Sat.) is a restaurant doubling as a bar that is popular with the expat crowd.

CNN and sports are on the cable TV, and the restaurant serves decent food, including the all-American staple breakfast of eggs, hash browns, bacon, and toast. Reilly's GuateCity (12 Calle 6-25 Zona 1, reillys.guatecity@gmail.com), a spin-off of the popular Irish pub in Antigua Guatemala, is also a good bet in downtown Guatemala City.

Zona Viva's motley assortment of upscale bars is constantly in flux. New places open and close all the time, and it's hard to keep up with all the changes, even if you live in Guatemala City. A classic expat hangout, Shakespeare's Pub (13 Calle and 1a Avenida, Torre Santa Clara II, Local 5, Zona 10, tel. 2331-2641, 11am-1am Mon.-Sat., 2pm-1am Sun.) appropriately advertises, "No tragedy, no comedy, just good times." Cheers (13 Calle 0-40 Zona 10, tel. 2368-2089, 9am-1am Mon.-Sat., 1pm-midnight Sun.) is a cool sports bar with scrumptious buffalo wings, frosty beer on tap, dartboards, pool tables, foosball, big-screen TVs, and classic rock on the stereo. Rattle N Hum (4a Avenida 16-11 Zona 10, noon-1am daily) is a fun, Australian-owned place often featuring live music. There's also tasty pub grub, and it's popular with locals and visitors alike.

Among the hotel bars, the InterContinental's Maya Lounge (14 Calle 2-51 Zona 10, tel. 2143-4444) bears mentioning for the cool vibe and chic modern-day Mayan decor. I also must note the bar at the Hard Rock Café Guatemala City (1a Avenida y 13 Calle Zona 10, Edificio Dubai Center, tel. 2332-3862, www.hardrock.com/cafes/guatemala-city, noon-12:30am Mon.-Sat., 11am-10pm Sun.) for its live music, the sheer variety and creativity of drink options, and the simple fact that it's one of the few places in Guatemala City with a cool outdoor patio bar. Antigua's popular Monoloco (16 Calle 1-01 Zona 10, CC Plaza Obelisco, tel. 2367-3283, www.restaurantemonoloco.com) now has a Guatemala City location with the same fun atmosphere and decent bar food.

Nightclubs

Like the bars, nightclubs are in constant flux, but here are some options that have been around for some time. In Zona 10, Kalhua (15 Calle and 1a Avenida, Zona 10, 8pm-3am Mon.-Sat., $5 cover) is one of Guatemala City's most popular clubs with a wealthy clientele and hip atmosphere spread out on four floors. I've had a great time dancing to electronica at The Box Lounge Groove (15 Calle y 4a Avenida, Zona 10, 5pm-1am Tues.-Sat.). It's on the small side, but its loyal clientele don't seem to mind squeezing in. SOMA Centro Cultural (11 Calle 4-27 Zona 1, tel. 2253-0406) is a good downtown option for music and a hip atmosphere. Also downtown, Savoy Zona Uno (12 Calle y Sexta Avenida 5-59 Zona 1, tel. 4040-4888) is wonderfully set in a derelict old building turned hipster haven.

There are street tacos and other munchies for sale on the ground floor.

Live Music

A popular place for live music in a wonderfully bohemian atmosphere is La Bodeguita del Centro (12 Calle 3-55 Zona 1, tel. 2230-1780, 8pm-2am Tues.-Sat., $4 cover on weekends). Besides live folk, rock, and jazz music, there are poetry readings, forums, and movies some nights. The atmosphere features posters the likes of Bob Marley and Che Guevara, as well as tons of Che-related memorabilia. Food is also served, with tasty chicken sandwiches. TrovaJazz (Vía 6 3-55 Zona 4, tel. 2267-9388, www.trovajazz.com) has live trova most evenings. It also serves food and coffee beverages. For live jazz, check out La Esquina Jazz Café (6a Avenida 0-15 Zona 2, tel. 2230-2859, noon-8pm Mon. and Thurs., noon-10pm Sat.-Sun).

PERFORMING ARTS

The Centro Cultural Miguel Ángel Asturias (24 Calle 3-81 Zona 4, tel. 2232-4042, 2232-4043, 2232-4044, or 2232-4045, mcd.gob.gt/teatro-nacional/) hosts ballet and a number of cultural events throughout the year. Check listings in the *Prensa Libre* newspaper

Hard Rock Café Guatemala City

or *Recrearte,* a free monthly publication widely available in tourist shops and hotels.

The **Teatro de la Cámara de la Industria** (Chamber of Industry Theater, Ruta 6, 9-21 Zona 4, tel. 2331-9191, showtimes 8:30pm Fri. and Sat., 5pm Sun., $8) usually has theater performances on weekends, mostly of satirical works.

For other cultural events, check the entertainment section of the useful Spanish-language website at www.deguate.com.

CINEMA

Guatemala City has a number of excellent movie theaters, with movies sometimes opening on the same day as their U.S. release. It's also (compared to the U.S.) a lot cheaper to go see a movie. The city's original IMAX movie theater is found at **Cines Pradera Concepción** (tel. 2329-2550, circuitoalba. com.gt), at the Pradera Concepción shopping mall along Km. 17.5 of Carretera a El Salvador, where you can have the IMAX theater experience for just $6. In one of the city's most popular shopping malls is **Cinépolis Miraflores** (Centro Comercial Miraflores, 21 Avenida 4-32 Zona 11, tel. 2378-2300, www.cinepolis. com.gt). Miraflores now also has an IMAX theater. Cinépolis (a Mexican chain) also has a location in Zona 10's **Oakland Mall** (Diagonal 6, 13-01 Zona 10, www.cinepolis.com.gt). Five of Oakland Mall's theaters are VIP lounges, in which you can order a meal and/or drink while you watch a movie. Other Cinépolis locations include **Cinépolis Cayalá** (Boulevard Rafael Landívar 10-05 Zona 16, Paseo Cayalá, tel. 2378-2300, www.cinepolis.com.gt) and **Cinépolis Portales** (Km. 4.5 Carretera al Atlántico Zona 17, Centro Comercial Portales, tel. 2378-2300, www.cinepolis.com.gt).

Not to be outdone, U.S. franchise Cinemark opened its first Guatemalan location at **Cinemark Eskala Roosevelt** (Calzada Roosevelt Km. 13.8 Zona 11, tel. 2250-7084, www.cinemarkca.com) featuring 3-D movies. There's a now a second location at **Cinemark Arkadia** (Boulevard Los Próceres, 18 Calle 26-21 Zona 10, www.cinemarkca.com) showing 3-D, D-BOX and XD movies.

Check the *Prensa Libre* newspaper or the theaters' websites for showtimes. Movies at all of these venues generally cost between $4 and $5, and all have stadium seating.

AMUSEMENT PARKS

The creators of Retalhuleu's (Pacific Coast) Xocomil and Xetulul theme parks have provided Guatemala City with a fun entertainment option in the form of **Mundo Petapa** (Avenida Petapa 42-36 Zona 12, tel. 2423-9000, www.irtra.org.gt, 9am-5pm Thurs.-Sat., 9am-6pm Sun., $13 adults, $7 children). There are plenty of rides (including a small roller coaster), swimming pools, a dinosaur-inspired playground, and a small zoo to keep kids and adults entertained. Food prices in the many kiosks and eateries are surprisingly reasonable for a theme park in an urban area. If adrenaline is your thing, check out **X Park** (Final Avenida Hincapié, Km. 11.5 Carretera a Boca del Monte, tel. 2380-2080, www.xpark. net, $2 admission, activities from $2.50), where there is bungee jumping, paintball, an obstacle course, and a climbing wall.

Have an outdoor adventure without going too far from Guatemala City at **Green Rush** (Km. 24 Carretera a El Salvador, tel. 5708-8801 or 5900-4291, www.greenrush.com.gt, 8am-8pm weekends, weekdays with prior reservation, $7 adults, $4 children; entrance includes access to trails, animal sanctuary, and relaxation areas). This ecoadventure park in the eastern hillsides flanking Guatemala City features 10 kilometers of trails and various outdoor activities that include archery ($2.50 and up), horseback riding ($2.50-13), and a zipline ($7). There's an animal sanctuary and a trail leading to a far-off waterfall. Services include a restaurant and picnic areas with gorgeous views over the Guatemala City valley. You can camp here with your own tent or go glamping in one of their souped-up safari tents ($121 d, including breakfast). The tents have private decks with lovely views and private bathrooms with hot-water showers.

Shopping

You can find almost anything you might possibly want or need in Guatemala City. In addition to many modern shopping malls stocked with the latest fashions and electronics, there are a number of department stores for household appliances and cosmetics. For grocery shopping, the local giant is Paiz, which was recently taken over by WalMart. La Torre is also a well-stocked local grocery chain. U.S.-style warehouse shopping is available at PriceSmart or at a number of local chains. Guatemalans love U.S.-made goods, which is easy to see given their wide availability. For organic grocery shopping and natural foods, head to Orgánica (Diagonal 6 16-23 Zona 10, tel. 2363-1819, 9am-7pm Mon.-Sat., and Km. 15.5 Carretera a El Salvador, Condado Concepción Fase 1 Local #21, tel. 6634-7077, 9am-6pm Mon.-Sat.). The website for all locations is www.organicastore.com.

CLOTHING STORES

In line with its fashionable cafés and expensive hotels, Guatemala City also features a number of attractive stores for window-shopping or picking up an outfit should you need something nice to wear for a fancy dinner or night out on the town. Two of the most fashionable retail outlets are the European chain Mexx (16 Calle 5-86 Zona 10, Plaza Magnolia, tel. 2368-0757, www.mexx.com, 10am-8pm daily) and the European-inspired menswear store Saúl Méndez (6a Avenida 15-64 Zona 10, tel. 2379-8722, www.saulemendez.com, 10am-8pm daily). Saúl Méndez, Mexx, and more recently, Zara (www.zara.com.gt), have locations in the following upscale shopping malls.

SHOPPING MALLS

Guatemala City has some excellent shopping malls carrying the most basic or most exclusive items one could need, in addition to fashionable boutiques and department stores. None of the latter (curiously) seem to result from Guatemalan investment. These include Simán (El Salvador), Carrion (Honduras), Figaly (Panama), and

Parque Comercial Las Majadas

Sears (United States). The city's largest shopping mall is **Pradera Concepción** (Km. 17.5 Carretera a El Salvador, 10am-7pm Mon.-Thurs. and 10am-9pm Fri.-Sat.), with a variety of familiar stores and restaurant chains including Sears and T.G.I. Friday's. It adjoins a smaller, open-air shopping center known as **Condado Concepción,** which features a Starbucks and an Applebee's in addition to several local chains. Opened in 2003 and expanded in 2006 and 2011, the sprawling **Galerías Miraflores** (21 Avenida 4-32 Zona 11, 10am-8pm Mon.-Thurs., 10am-9pm Fri.-Sat., 10am-7pm Sun.) also harbors some of Guatemala's most exclusive stores, including a Simán department store, the international Zara boutique, and a L'Occitane store. There's also an IHOP if you need your pancake fix. Across the way is the **Parque Comercial Las Majadas** shopping center with a Sears, Fetiche perfume store, and a T.G.I. Friday's. They've recently expanded with a new, very pleasant outdoor concept known as **Majadas ONCE** (tel. 2200-9696, www.majadas.com, 9am-9pm daily).

In Zona 10, east up the hill toward the Carretera a El Salvador, is **Galerías La Pradera** (20 Calle 25-85 Zona 10, tel. 2367-4136, 10am-8pm Mon.-Sat. and 10am-7pm Sun.), an upscale shopping mall remodeled in 2010-2011. Though not as upscale as its Zona Viva location might suggest, **Gran Centro Los Próceres** (16 Calle 2-00 Zona 10, tel. 2332-8742) nonetheless is conveniently situated near the major Zona 10 hotels. Also conveniently situated in Zona 10 (and brand-new) is **Arkadia Shopping** (Boulevard Los Próceres, 18 Calle 26-21 Zona 10, www.arkadiashopping.com, 10am-8pm Sun.-Thurs., 10am-9pm Fri.-Sat.).

Zona 10's most upscale shopping mall is also Guatemala City's nicest. **Oakland Mall** (Diagonal 6, 13-01 Zona 10, www.oakland-mall.com.gt, 10am-8pm Mon.-Thurs., 10am-9pm Fri.-Sat., 10am-7pm Sun.) features 170 stores spread across three floors, in addition to several movie theaters. Among its stores

the open-air style of Paseo Cayalá

and restaurants you'll find an aquarium, an impressive waterfall producing geometric shapes, and even a carousel imported from Italy. A Starbucks with plenty of outdoor seating fronts the street along its main entrance. Also in this sector is the very pleasant **Plaza Fontabella** (4a Ave. 12-59 Zona 10, tel. 6628-8600, www.plazafontabella.com), built as an outdoor mall in neocolonial style, where you can enjoy Guatemala's spring-like climate and a decent selection of stores and restaurants while strolling the cobblestone pedestrian walkways. Guatemala's first Carolina Herrera designer handbag store opened here in 2011. Convenient for shoppers coming in from neighboring Antigua due to its location on the southwestern edges of Guatemala City is **SanKris Mall** (Boulevard Principal de San Cristóbal, tel. 2300-0600, www.sankris.com.gt, 10am-8pm daily). It has a decent selection of stores and a World Gym.

In Zona 16, you'll find a fine example of the recent trend toward construction of outdoor pedestrian malls in warm-weather locales. **Paseo Cayalá** (Ciudad Cayalá, Zona 16, www.paseocayala.com.gt) is housed in a sprawling collection of whitewashed Spanish neocolonial buildings. There are numerous specialty stores in addition to cool restaurants and bars with outdoor patio seating fronting the cobblestone pedestrian thoroughfare. Three universities lie nearby, and the shopping district is part of a larger residential complex encompassing homes and student apartments. Recent additions include a movie theater, driving range, a World Gym, and a Starbucks. There are lovely views of the city's downtown core, off in the distance.

HANDICRAFTS

You can shop the jam-packed stalls in downtown Guatemala City's **Mercado Central** (8a Avenida and 6a Calle, 6am-6pm Mon.-Sat., 9am-noon Sun.) for textiles, *típica* clothing, and leather goods. A safer and more enjoyable option can be found near the airport and Zona 13 museums at the open-air **Mercado de Artesanías** (Boulevard Juan Pablo II, 8am-6pm Mon.-Sat., 8am-1pm Sun.), with a fairly wide assortment of handicrafts and tourist souvenirs.

Recommended retailers include **Lin Canola** (5a Calle 9-60 Zona 1, tel. 2232-0858, www.lin-canola.com, 9am-6pm Mon.-Fri.), where the assortment varies from home decorative items to jewelry and everything between. This store is especially recommended if you want to buy Guatemalan fabrics by the yard. Its Zona 10 location, **In Nola** (18 Calle 21-31 Zona 10, Boulevard Los Próceres, tel. 2367-2424, 8:30am-6:30pm Mon.-Fri. and 8:30am-1:30pm Sat.), is more modern and contains much the same in a better part of town.

Selling fashionable adaptations on traditional designs for the home, **Textura** (Diagonal 6, 13-63 Zona 10, tel. 2367-2098, 9:30am-7pm Mon.-Fri.., 9:30am-2:30pm Sat.) is especially recommended for its beautiful and colorful hammocks.

ART GALLERIES

If you want to take in the work of local artists, head to Guatemala's oldest art gallery, **Galería El Túnel** (16 Calle 1-01 Zona 10, Plaza Obelisco, tel. 2367-3284, www.galeriaeltunel.com.gt), featuring the work of more than 100 artists. Another good art gallery worth checking out is **el attico** (4a Avenida 15-45 Zona 14, tel. 2368-0853, www.elattico.com). **Fundación Rozas Botrán** (16 Calle 4-66 Zona 14, tel. 2366-7064, www.fundacionrozasbotran.org) has rotating painting, sculpture, and photography exhibits in its spacious gallery.

BOOKS

For a great atmosphere for unwinding with a cup of coffee or tea and a large selection of books (though mostly in Spanish), try **Sophos** (Plaza Fontabella, 4a Ave. 12-59 Zona 10, tel. 2419-7070, www.sophosenlinea.com, 9am-8pm Mon.-Sat., 10am-6pm Sun.). Also with plenty of books in Spanish is **Artemis Edinter** (www.artemisedinter.com) with several locations including Galerías Miraflores, Pradera Concepción, and Oakland Mall.

A number of bookstores cater to the expat community, stocking a variety of English-language books on their shelves. **Vista Hermosa Book Shop** (2a Calle 18-50, Vista Hermosa II, Zona 15, tel. 2369-1003, vhbookshop@intelnet.net.gt, 9am-1pm and 2pm-6pm Mon.-Sat.) has books in English and Spanish and is in a quiet residential sector east of Zona 10.

OUTDOOR GEAR

For anything you may have neglected to bring for your outdoor Guatemala adventures, head to **Big Mountain** (Centro Comercial Miraflores, 2do nivel, Kiosko K-96, tel. 2474-8547, www.bigmountainonline.com, 9am-8pm Mon.-Sun.), offering a good assortment of hiking, climbing, mountain biking, and camping gear, and name-brand outdoor clothing.

Another option for outdoor gear is The North Face (2nd floor of the Oakland Mall, Diagonal 6, 13-01 Zona 10, tel. 2336-6881, 10am-8pm Mon.-Thurs., 10am-9pm Fri.-Sat., 10am-7pm Sun.). There's also now a location at the Galerías Miraflores shopping mall.

Recreation

PARKS

The idea of a greenbelt is relatively new to Guatemalan city planners. Most of the city's parks tend to be plazas centered around churches. A refreshing alternative is that of Parque Ecológico Deportivo Cayalá (Calzada de la Paz, Zona 16, in front of the Cemaco warehouse, tel. 4561-8082 or 5744-4360, www.cayala.org, 8am-5:30pm Tues.-Sun., $5), where there are nature trails winding through the park's 24 acres of mostly forested land showcasing the flora and fauna of the city's *barrancos*. The urban oasis is privately run by ecological organization FUNDAECO and entry includes a visit to the Museo Metropolitano de Aves (Metropolitan Bird Museum). The museum showcases wooden versions of Guatemala's myriad bird species, including endemic and migratory birds.

On Sunday mornings, parts of Avenida Las Américas and Avenida La Reforma (from Plaza Eucarística to Plaza Israel) are closed to car traffic as part of the municipality's Pasos y Pedales initiative. Pedestrians, cyclists, inline skaters, and skateboarders take to the broad streets, while the green grass and plazas of the boulevards' wide central dividers serve as pleasant areas for rest and relaxation. A more recent development is the addition of a bike path running down the entire length of the wide, tree-and-grass strewn median of Avenida La Reforma all the way from Plaza El Obelisco to its northern extreme.

HEALTH CLUBS

There are a number of good gymnasiums, mostly U.S. franchises, where you can pay a day rate of about $7 to work out if you don't have a membership. World Gym (www.worldgym.com.gt) has four locations to choose from. Its Calzada Roosevelt location (Calzada Roosevelt 21-09 Zona 7, Centro Comercial Gran Vía Roosevelt, tel. 2475-2856) is conveniently across the street from Galerías Miraflores and the Grand Tikal Futura hotel. It also has a Zona 10 location (Boulevard Los Próceres 25-74 Zona 10, Gran Vía Pradera, tel. 2423-6000), a third location in the southwest suburbs of San Cristóbal (3ra. Calle Sector A-3, Boulevard San Cristóbal 6-72 Zona 8 de Mixco, SanKris Mall, tel. 2424-4848), and the newest location at Paseo Cayalá (Diagonal 35 Boulevard Austriaco 16-25 Zona 16, Cardales de Cayalá, tel. 2491-4333). All have a full gym and swimming pool. You can also work out at Gold's Gym (Pradera Concepción Mall, Km. 17.5 Carretera a El Salvador, tel. 6634-1240, www.goldsgym.com).

GOLF

Fans of golf will find some excellent golf courses in and around the city; those within private country clubs are usually still open to visitors. You can enjoy a round of golf surrounded by the country's spectacular mountain scenery as you play on narrow, sloping fairways lined with pine trees and a variety of other obstacles. Several of sportfishing outfitters have combined fishing and golf packages. If interested, contact The Great Sailfishing Company (tel. 7934-6220, or 877/763-0851 U.S., www.greatsailfishing.com) or Sailfish Bay Lodge (tel. 2426-3909 direct or 800/638-7405 U.S. reservations, www.sailfishbay.com). It's also possible to arrange a round of golf through the concierges at some of the city's finer hotels, including the Westin Camino

Real and InterContinental. Entry to all of these clubs is by prior authorization only. You'll need to call ahead or email.

In 2006 and 2007, Guatemala City's San Isidro Golf Club hosted the NGA/Hooter's Pro Golf Tour, which has become an annual event between the last week of February and the first week of March. Guatemala is also a major stop along the annual Tour de las Américas in February.

Guatemala City's exclusive Cayalá area is now home to a driving range, the first of its kind in Central America. Top Tee (Boulevard Austríaco 37-01, Arcadia de Cayalá, Zona 16, tel. 2300-0700, www.toptee.com.gt) has 38 driving stations, TV lounges for watching sports, and a well-stocked bar.

San Isidro Golf Club

Still officially within the city limits in Zona 16, San Isidro Golf Club (Finca San Isidro, Zona 16, tel. 2419-1200, www.clubcampestresanisidro.com) is the city's most modern and is in a quiet residential section in its eastern extremes. The 18-hole, par-72 course measures 6,640 yards and offers some truly spectacular views of Guatemala City flanked by Agua, Acatenango, and Fuego Volcanoes. Greens fees are $75, clubs rent for $15, a cart rental costs $20, and caddies are $15. The splendid facilities here include a restaurant overlooking the greens featuring a beautiful dining room with vaulted wooden ceiling, a gym, a squash court, and a swimming pool with lap lanes.

Hacienda Nueva Country Club

The 18-hole, 7,100-yard, par-72 golf course at Hacienda Nueva Country Club (Km. 25, Ruta Nacional 18, Carretera a Mataquescuintla, San José Pinula, tel. 6628-1000, www.haciendanueva.com, $75 Tues.-Fri., $90 weekends and holidays) is just outside the city near Carretera a El Salvador and set beautifully on the grounds of a 16th-century Jesuit monastery. There's a small chapel with original artwork where Mass is still held weekly. Facilities include nine tennis courts, two squash courts, tennis and golf pro shops, and a swimming pool that has won international design awards. The clubhouse has three dining areas, including a poolside snack bar, a casual dining room serving international dishes, and La Pérgola, an outdoor steakhouse overlooking the 18th hole. Fees include $15 for caddie service and $25 for cart rental. A limited number of golf clubs are available for rental at $15. There are also a driving range and putting green.

Alta Vista Golf and Tennis Club

The most challenging course can be found just down the road from Hacienda Nueva at Alta Vista Golf and Tennis Club (Km. 27, Ruta Nacional 18, Carretera a Mataquescuintla, San José Pinula, tel. 6661-1414, www.altavistagolf.com.gt, 7am-8pm Tues.-Sun., $75), where the 18-hole, par-71, slope-122 course is divided into two nine-hole sections. Additional challenges include 74 sand traps and two water traps with a route defined by 1,800 trees of varying species, adding a nice alpine touch to the incredible mountain views. The clubhouse is in a large and attractive three-story, English-style building with an elegant restaurant, a bar with pool table, an indoor swimming pool, three squash courts, and six tennis courts. Golf cart rentals cost $30, clubs are $15, and caddies $15.

Mayan Golf Course

South of the city in the neighboring district of Villa Nueva, Mayan Golf Course (Finca El Zarzal, Villa Nueva, tel. 6685-5800, www.mayangolfclub.com, $75) is Guatemala City's oldest, dating to 1918. The facilities here feel somewhat dated but have been well maintained. The 18-hole, par-72 golf course has exquisite views of Lake Amatitlán and Pacaya Volcano along its 7,092-yard length. Rental clubs and golf carts are available, and there is a café with a terrace overlooking the course. Additional sporting facilities include a bowling alley, tennis courts, a soccer field, volleyball court, and swimming pool.

Alta Vista Golf and Tennis Club offers one of Guatemala's most challenging courses.

BOWLING

Metro Bowl (2a Calle 15-93 Zona 15, on Vista Hermosa Boulevard, tel. 2243-2424, www.metrobowl.com.gt) is Central America's largest bowling alley, with 28 lanes. There are also eight pool tables and an area for video games. And, of course, there's a snack bar.

HORSEBACK RIDING/ EQUESTRIAN

Equestrian has become increasingly popular with Guatemala's well-to-do. In addition to the recently rehabilitated horse track known as **Parque Deportivo Ecuestre La Aurora**, next to the airport in Zona 13, there are a number of private facilities where equestrian and horseback riding are practiced. **Guate Equinos** (www.guateequinos.com, tel. 3163-8160 and 5305-7443) offers horseback riding lessons for all ages and instruction in all things equestrian on the grounds of the horse track at La Aurora and at its own facilities near a turnoff at km. 24.3 Carretera a El Salvador. Call or visit the website for a map of how to get here. **Club Ecuestre Vista Hermosa** (20 Avenida 21-00 Zona 16, Jacarandas de Cayalá, tel. 2261-0926, www.

clubecuestrevistahermosa.com) has three different tracks at its facility in Guatemala City's Cayalá area. For more on this sport of rising popularity in Guatemala, check out the Asociación Nacional de Ecuestres de Guatemala online at www.guatecuestres.com.

SPECTATOR SPORTS

Like other Latin Americans, Guatemalans are crazy about *fútbol*. The two most popular teams in the country's four-team national soccer league, denoted by the colors of their jerseys, are the Rojos (Municipales) and Cremas (Comunicaciones), who usually end up battling it out at the end of the season for the championship title. International games are also a big event, as Guatemala has never been to a World Cup. In recent years, it has gotten closer than it's ever been, and the postgame celebrations have spilled into the streets and lasted into the wee hours of the morning. Unfortunately, their high hopes have ended in bitter disappointment. Games can be seen at the **Estadio Mateo Flores** (10a Avenida, Zona 5), but be advised: The scene can get quite rowdy. In 1996, things got so out of hand that a stampede ensued when stands collapsed, killing 100 people. The soccer stadium has been remodeled in the aftermath. If you've always wanted to see a Latin American soccer match, you might want to check it out.

You can see baseball games at Parque Minerva's ballpark (Zona 2).

CITY TOURS

Traditional city tours can be arranged through any of the larger hotels or via **Clark Tours** (7a Avenida 14-76, Plaza Clark, Zona 9, tel. 2412-4700, www.clarktours.com). It has offices in the Westin Camino Real, Holiday Inn, and Barceló. For an urban adventure exploring Guatemala City on the ground level, consider a **bicycle tour** offered by local hostel **Quetzalroo** (6a Avenida 7-84 Zona 10, tel. 5746-0830, www.quetzalroo.com, $15

including bike rental). The tour varies depending on guests' interests and needs but you can expect to cover a lot of ground and see some interesting attractions through the eyes of well-informed local guide Marcos Romero-Close. The long version of the tour traverses Zonas 1, 2, 4, 10, 13, and 14 with stops at art galleries, coffee shops, a Zacapa Rum retail outlet, the Civic Center, Paseo de la Sexta, and various museums. Although Zona 10's Avenida La Reforma has a bike trail, most of the tour takes place on the gritty streets and sidewalks of Guatemala City. Helmets and reflective vests are provided. It's surprisingly safer on Guatemala City streets than you have been led to believe and Marcos has even hosted celebrities on the tour, including well-known Mexican singer Julieta Venegas.

Accommodations

Guatemala City has a wide variety of accommodations for all budgets. The major U.S. hotel chains have properties in Zonas 10, 11, and 13—close to the airport. Downtown is home to many of the city's budget accommodations.

CENTRO HISTÓRICO
$50-100

There are some real cheapies in downtown Guatemala City, traditionally the city's budget accommodation headquarters, though there are also some nice budget options outside the downtown area now, so there's really very little reason to stay in this somewhat dodgy part of town.

An exception located on a quiet side street is ★ **Posada Belén Museum Inn** (13 Calle "A" 10-30 Zona 1, tel. 2251-3478, www.posadabelen.com, $55-67 d), an 1873 home converted into a lovely museum inn. It has 10 rooms with tile floors tastefully decorated with Guatemalan bedspreads, paintings, and weavings. Its gracious hosts, René and Francesca, speak English and can help you

plan your journeys into Guatemala's rugged interior. Amenities include telephone and Internet access. All rooms have private bath and rates include breakfast. Other delicious homemade meals are available upon request. Oozing with history is the landmark **Hotel Pan American** (9a Calle 5-63 Zona 1, tel. 2232-6807, www.hotelpanamerican.com.gt, $55 d), which was once Guatemala City's go-to property, having been established by its namesake airline. Rooms have tile floors and are nicely decorated with Guatemalan artwork and furnishings. The dining room, serving international and Guatemalan dishes, is well known for its antique charm and elegance, with waiters wearing traditional village attire. It's also very well located, just steps away from bustling Paseo de la Sexta.

ZONA 4
$50-100

Conquistador Hotel (Vía 5, 4-68 Zona 4, tel. 2424-4444, hotelconquistador.com.gt, $90 d, including breakfast) was formerly a Ramada property. You'll find a lobby bar, the

Café Jardín serving a breakfast and lunch buffet, and La Pérgola serving fine international dishes for dinner.

ZONA 9
$50-100
The Howard Johnson Inn (Avenida La Reforma 4-22 Zona 9, tel. 2201-1111, www. hojo.com.gt, $95-103 d) comes with all the standard amenities you would expect from this international hotel chain, including air-conditioning, fan, nice wooden furniture, phone, and TV. There's a small restaurant in the lobby. Try to get a room facing the outside street.

$100-200
Among Guatemala City's numerous international hotel chain options is ★ Barceló Guatemala City (7a Avenida 15-45 Zona 9, tel. 800/227-2356, www.barceloguatemalacity.com, $125 d), with six different room types to choose from and all the standard comforts usually found in the Spanish hotel chain's properties. American and United Airlines have offices in the lobby of this former Marriott property.

The Hilton Garden Inn Guatemala City (13 Calle 7-65 Zona 9, tel. 2423-0909, http:// hiltongardeninn3.hilton.com, from $119 d) is a winner for its sophisticated modern ambience. Amenities include a gym and restaurant. Its 110 rooms have air-conditioning.

ZONA 10
Under $50
The current Guatemala City favorite of the backpacking crowd is ★ Quetzalroo Hostel (6a Avenida 7-84 Zona 10, tel. 5746-0830, www.quetzalroo.com, $16-35). The owners take great pride in sharing their vast knowledge and enthusiasm for Guatemala and its capital city with visitors. For $16, you get a comfortable bed in a dorm room, shared bath, free wireless Internet, continental breakfast and free shuttle transport to the airport nearby. Private rooms with shared bath cost

$35 d per night. The hostel is conveniently situated in the heart of the Zona Viva. A fun add-on is a historical bike tour of Guatemala City. There's a cool rooftop patio with city views.

$50-100
Best Western Plus Hotel Stofella (2a Avenida 12-28 Zona 10, tel. 2410-8600, www. stofella.com, $100 d), a solid choice for business travelers, has rooms with fan or air-conditioning with breakfast included in the nightly rate. You'll find a lobby lounge, a fitness room with whirlpool tub, a bar, and in-room Internet connection. Offering many of the same services as its pricier sister hotels under the management of the Camino Real chain, Biltmore Express (15 Calle 0-31 Zona 10, tel. 2338-5000, hotelbiltmore.com.gt, $90 d) offers a continental breakfast and has comfortable rooms with broadband Internet. Guests can enjoy use of the nearby Westin Camino Real's swimming pool, whirlpool tub, and tennis and racquetball courts for an additional $10 a day. There's a free shuttle to and from the airport.

$100-200
Otelito (12 Calle 4-51 Zona 10, tel. 2339-1811, www.otelito.com, $140-200 d) is cool and hip but a bit noisy for some people's taste on account of a popular lobby lounge and nightclubs in its vicinity. There are 12 rooms, all named after local produce, housed in a modern home turned upscale hotel. The decor is minimalist with a different color scheme in evidence during each of the year's four seasons. It offers chill-out music playing on the speakers throughout the property, wireless Internet throughout, a business center, and a book exchange. Rooms feature nice artwork, 300-thread-count Egyptian cotton sheets, down pillows, air-conditioning, flat-screen cable TV, hardwood floors, and in-room chill-out music. Some have a mini-fridge. Walk-in showers feature tempered glass in lieu of shower curtains. There's a hip,

frosted-glass lounge and restaurant (lunch and dinner daily, $7-12) downstairs. Popular Plaza Fontabella shopping mall is right across the street.

A top choice is the fabulous, 246-room ★ **Real InterContinental Guatemala** (14 Calle 2-51 Zona 10, tel. 2413-4444 or 800/835-4654 toll-free U.S., www.intercontinental.com, $125-485 d) with a wonderful lobby featuring Guatemalan paintings and sculpture, a sushi restaurant, a French café, and *boulangerie* and patisserie. The comfortable, stylish rooms feature in-room Internet access, down pillows, Egyptian cotton sheets, and flat-screen cable TV. Bathrooms have rain showerheads, and the safe deposit boxes are large enough to accommodate a laptop. There are free airport shuttles and a pleasant swimming pool on a deck overlooking the city. President George W. Bush and his wife, Laura, spent the night here during their 24-hour visit to Guatemala in March 2007.

Mercure Casa Veranda (12 Calle 1-24 Zona 10, tel. 2411-4100, www.mercure.com, $120 d) features all the amenities you'd come to expect from a reputable international hotel chain. Among the unique features of the property's 99 spacious suites are hardwood floors, Persian rugs, wireless Internet, and balconies with fantastic city views; some suites have full kitchens. The property also features a decent restaurant and bar.

A number of other international hotel chains are in this price category. Among them is the ever-reliable **Holiday Inn** (1a Avenida 13-22 Zona 10, tel. 2421-0000 or 800/009-9900 toll-free U.S., www.hinn.com.gt, $120 d), the landmark 271-room **Westin Camino Real** (14 Calle and Avenida La Reforma Zona 10, tel. 2333-3000, www.starwoodhotels.com, $149-329 d), and the business traveler-oriented, all-suite **Viva Clarion Suites** (tel. 2421-3333, www.clarionguatemala.com, $105-125 d).

The **Radisson** (1a Avenida 12-46 Zona 10, tel. 2421-5151 or 800/333-3333 toll-free U.S., www.radisson.com, $120 d) is another good business traveler option. All rooms have a minibar, in-room safe, large windows with city views, and in-room Internet access. There are also a gym, sauna, business center, and sushi restaurant/bar open 11am-midnight daily.

Conveniently near the U.S. embassy in a building oozing with European charm, **Hotel**

view of Zona 10 from the rooftop of Quetzalroo Hostel

San Carlos (Avenida La Reforma 7-89, Zona 10, tel. 2247-3000, www.hsancarlos.com, $90-175 d) offers 23 modern, comfortable rooms. The spacious suites are a good value and have hardwood floors and kitchenettes. There are also one- or two-bedroom apartments. At research time, U.S. hotel chains **Hyatt Place, Courtyard by Marriott,** and **La Quinta** announced plans for Guatemala City hotels to open in Zona 10 in 2016. The Hyatt Place project is particularly interesting, as it's part of a mixed use commercial, office, and residential complex known as AVIA encompassing three towers built round a plaza dotted with exuberant greenery. It will take up an entire city block, between 2nd and 3a Avenidas and 11 and 12 Calles.

ZONA 11
$100-200

Formerly the city's Hyatt Regency, the **Grand Tikal Futura** (Calzada Roosevelt 22-43 Zona 11, tel. 2410-0800, www.grand-tikalfutura.com.gt, $90-600 d) maintains high-quality standards and has comfortable, well-furnished rooms varying from standard rooms to stunning Diplomatic Suites. All have splendid views of the city and surrounding mountains. Restaurants include elegant La Molienda, serving international and Guatemalan dishes for breakfast, lunch, and dinner and the excellent Asia Grill and Wok serving lunch and dinner in a tropically inspired, casual atmosphere. There is a lobby bar, a fitness center with health-food bar, and a covered swimming pool with poolside service and city views.

ZONA 13 (AIRPORT)
Under $50

A number of inexpensive hotels all offering similar services are centered in a middle-class neighborhood near the airport. All offer free transport to and from the terminal as well as breakfast, though this varies from continental minimalist to a full-on Guatemalan feast. **Guatefriends B&B** (16

Calle 7-40 Zona 13, Aurora 1, tel. 5308-3275, $20) is run by a friendly couple. The rooms and property are decorated in bright colors that nod to Guatemala's colorful textiles and vivid Mayan culture. Among the nice extras are tasty home-cooked meals. **Dos Lunas Guest House** (21 Calle 10-92 Zona 13, Aurora II, tel. 2261-4248, www.hoteldoslunas.com, $18 pp) has nine basic rooms, all with shared bath, including a breakfast of eggs and toast. Reservations are necessary, as it's usually booked. **Hostal Los Lagos** (8a Avenida 15-85 Zona 13, tel. 2261-2809, www.loslagoshostal.com, starting $30 pp) has cheerful rooms with colorful paintings and several beds each. Rates include a complete breakfast of eggs and beans or cereal, and coffee or tea. You'll find Internet, cable TV, laundry, and baggage storage as well as two sitting rooms with bamboo furniture.

A notch above the rest of the lodgings in the airport neighborhood is ★ **Hostal Villa Toscana** (16 Calle 8-20, Aurora I, Zona 13, tel. 2261-2854, www.hostalvillatoscana.com, $52-68 d), a bed-and-breakfast where there are large, well-decorated rooms with private bathrooms and wireless Internet—there is even a suite with a balcony and volcano views. **Hotel Casa Blanca Inn** (15 Calle "C" 7-35, Aurora I, Zona 13, tel. 2261-3116, www.hotelcasablancainn.com, $40-55 d) is another good choice with pleasant, simply decorated rooms with big beds, reading lamps, and shared or private bathrooms. There is wireless Internet throughout and a pleasant patio bar.

$100-200

The 183-room **Crowne Plaza** (Avenida Las Américas 9-08 Zona 13, tel. 2422-5050 or 800/835-4654 toll-free U.S., www.ihg.com, $115 d) features rooms with the chain's Sleep Advantage, including deliciously comfortable beds, fine duvets, and your choice of seven different pillows. It has a business center with wireless Internet, a huge gym with excellent city views from the top floor, a sports bar with video poker and slot machines, and a heated

view from the Presidential Suite at Vista Real Guatemala

pool with whirlpool tub. The Los Volcanes restaurant, on the ground floor, serves international and local dishes à la carte or buffet style. There's a piano player at night. **Video Lotería Monte Carlo** (video gambling, 1pm-3am daily) is also based on the ground floor, featuring video poker and slot machines. Proceeds benefit the environmental foundation Monte Carlo Verde.

CARRETERA A EL SALVADOR (SUBURBS)
$100-200

Although a bit far from the action, the all-suite ★ **Vista Real Guatemala** (Km. 8.5 Carretera a El Salvador, tel. 2420-7720, www.vistareal.com, from $119 d) scores big points for its location on a bluff overlooking the city and its neocolonial architecture featuring Mexican artistic touches. Its 129 rooms are all comfortable and well furnished with some truly splendid features, including vaulted wooden ceilings and neocolonial archways in some rooms. The Suite Gran Clase rooms are a good value and substantially nicer than the Master Suites, which are only slightly less expensive. Check the website for special deals. Wireless Internet is offered throughout the property. There is a pleasant, though unheated, garden swimming pool. Its Restaurante Las Ventanas is one of the city's most exclusive, with a variety of international dishes served in an elegant dining room overlooking the hotel's gardens. Its well-stocked Bar Quinta Real is open 5pm-1am Monday-Saturday.

Well outside of Guatemala City but entirely worth the trip, ★ **San Gregorio Hotel & Spa** (Carretera a Santa Elena Barillas Km. 29.5, tel. 6634-3666, www.sangregoriospa.com, $120 d) is a modern, ecochic facility with 10 stylish rooms featuring hardwood floors, flat-screen TVs, Guatemalan textiles, wood accents, and views over Guatemala City valley to Lake Amatitlán and Agua Volcano. There's an indoor/outdoor swimming pool; the hotel's ecochic status is punctuated by the use of solar panels for water heating and rainwater collection for landscape irrigation. To get here, take the Carretera a El Salvador to a turnoff at Km. 25. You'll see a Texaco gas station; follow the road to Santa Elena Barillas another 4.5 kilometers. A sign for San Gregorio indicates the intersection where you'll make a right-hand turn to the lodge.

Food

Cosmopolitan Guatemala City features a variety of excellent eating establishments for every taste and budget, as well as some more familiar U.S. franchises. In recent years, Jake's received a spot on *Travel + Leisure* magazine's list of Top 10 Restaurants in Latin America.

CAFÉS

A profusion of new cafés has come and gone in the downtown area in recent years. Among those still in business is Café de Imeri (6a Calle 3-34 Zona 1, tel. 2232-3722, www.de-imeri.com, 8am-6:30pm Mon.-Sat.), which enjoys a loyal following owed to its delightful old-fashioned atmosphere and efficiently elegant service. The cakes and baked goods are top-notch, and there are good breakfasts, tacos, pasta, and salads. It makes a great place for lunch with a set menu for $4.

Saúl Café (several locations throughout the city in Miraflores, Oakland Mall, and Paseo Cayalá, www.saulemendez.com/site/es/gastronomia.html, $8-15) is a local chain serving delicious sweet and salty crepes, ice cream, sandwiches, salads, smoothies, and coffee in an eclectic atmosphere with relaxing music. Beer and wine are also served. Caffé dei Fiori (15 Avenida 15-66 Zona 10, tel. 2363-5888, www.caffedeifiori.com, $3-8) has been around since the 1970s in three prior Zona 10 locations. Its current incarnation features a pleasant covered patio where breakfasts, pizzas, pastas, salads, and sandwiches are served. Desserts include delicious tiramisu and *empanadas de piña*. Great espresso drinks round out the meal.

There are a number of local coffee shops with a widespread presence throughout Guatemala City. These include & Café and Café Barista. If you must, there are four Starbucks locations in upscale Guatemala City shopping malls.

LIGHT MEALS AND SWEETS

Popular with Guatemalans, San Martin and Company (13 Calle 1-62 Zona 10 and various locations in upscale shopping malls, www.sanmartinbakery.com/english, 6am-8pm Mon.-Sat.) is a bakery and café with pleasant outdoor seating on a terrace or ceiling fan-cooled dining room inside. There are scrumptious croissant sandwiches for breakfast as well as a variety of sandwiches, salads, and soups for lunch and dinner in the $3-5 range.

Chocolate lovers will find bliss at Xocoli (6a Avenida 9-19 Zona 10, tel. 2362-3251, www.xocoli.com, 8:30am-6:30pm Mon.-Fri., 9am-1pm Sat.). The Mayan world is, after all, the birthplace of chocolate, dating back to the use of cacao beans as currency in Mayan times. Quite possibly the best artisanal gelato outside of Italy, Ríbola Gelato (Plaza Vista Muxbal local 109, Km. 9.5 Antigua Carretera a El Salvador, tel. 6646-6948, www.ribola.com.gt) serves a variety of mouthwatering flavors made with ingredients imported from Italy.

SPANISH

At Tapas y Cañas (13 Calle 7-78 Zona 10, tel. 2388-2700, www.tapasycanas.com, lunch and dinner daily) you can savor delicious Spanish tapas. Try the *pinchos españoles* or the *albondigas de lomito*. A longtime local favorite, ★ Altuna (5a Avenida 12-31 Zona 1, tel. 2251-7185 and 10a Calle 0-45 Zona 10, tel. 2332-6576, www.restaurantealtuna.com, noon-10pm Tues.-Sat., noon-5pm Sun., $7-22) is also one of the city's fanciest offerings with impeccable service and an elegant atmosphere. Specialties include fish and seafood dishes, including paella and lobster, but the restaurant also serves land-based fare, including *jamón serrano* and chorizo.

Pollo Campero and the Cult of Fried Chicken

If, like most people traveling home from Guatemala, you fly out on a commercial airline, don't be surprised by the distinct smell of fried chicken onboard your aircraft. One look at the overhead bins will quickly reveal that they are crammed tight with boxes of fried chicken. Meet Pollo Campero, which, along with coffee and bananas, may be one of Guatemala's main exports.

Guatemalans have always had an affinity for the stuff. It's actually quite good, though I've never taken it along as a carry-on. Many travelers take a box home for homesick relatives craving a taste of the land they left behind. Although Pollo Campero has opened up shop in recent years in several U.S. cities, expatriate Guatemalans still make a point of stopping at the store in La Aurora Airport to pick up a box. To illustrate the utter hold it has on the Guatemalan masses, the airport shop operated out of a streetside trailer during the airport's recent renovation at a time when all other businesses were simply closed.

You may be asked by U.S. Customs if you're carrying food, and this question might specifically address your smuggling of Pollo Campero. Rest assured, customs officials are happy to let the cooked chicken cross the American threshold after applying the requisite X-rays. Some Newark Airport customs officers even claim to have the uncanny ability to distinguish chicken from a Guatemalan Pollo Campero versus that of a San Salvador outlet, though I've never taken them up on offers to verify their claims.

Pollo Campero is becoming more than just a Guatemalan phenomenon, however. An aggressive company expansion includes the opening of numerous new locations throughout North America, Europe, and even Asia in the coming years. In 2007, Campero opened outlets in Jakarta, Indonesia, and Shanghai, China, with ambitious goals to open 500 more restaurants in China by 2012. Campero already operates 220 restaurants in 10 countries, including 38 in the United States. It employs more than 7,000 people and is the largest fast-food chain in Latin America. With such aggressive expansion plans, Pollo Campero may be headed for a location near you, and I don't mean seat 25F.

STEAKHOUSES

You'll find a variety of excellent steakhouses in Guatemala City, including **Hacienda Real** (5a Avenida 14-67 Zona 10, tel. 2380-8383, www.hacienda-real.com, lunch and dinner daily, $10-20), where the meals are served with tasty tortillas and savory side sauces. Try the peppered steak. There are other locations at Condado Concepción and Las Majadas. For absolutely astounding views of the city from its perch along Carretera a El Salvador, you can't top **El Portal del Ángel** (Km. 11.2 Carretera a El Salvador, tel. 2322-7300, www.elportaldelangel.net, noon-9pm Mon.-Thurs., noon-10pm Fri.-Sun., $8-35). The food is just as good as the views and the tasteful decor, with walls in vivid hues adorned with cool paintings of Catholic saints, make this place truly heavenly. It is also in Zona 11 at Paseo Miraflores and Zona 10 at Plaza Fontabella,

minus the city views. ★ **Don Emiliano** (4a Ave. 12-70 Zona 10, Oakland Mall; tel. 2475-5957, www.donemiliano.com.gt, noon-9pm Mon.-Thurs., noon-10pm Sun., $25) is another fine steakhouse with additional locations at Miraflores and the Mercado de Artesanías in Zona 13. It scores big points for its modern atmosphere and the beautiful presentation of its dishes. Try the tasty steak salads.

MEXICAN

Los Cebollines (6a Avenida 9-75 Zona 1, tel. 2232-7750 and Condado Concepción, at Km. 15.5 Carretera a El Salvador, tel. 6634-5405; www.cebollines.com, 7am-11pm Mon.-Thurs., 7am-midnight Fri.-Sat., 7am-10pm Sun.) serves tasty grilled meats, enchiladas, and tacos you can wash down with refreshing lemonades, smoothies, or cocktails. Try the delicious *tacos de pollo pibil*. Along with its branch in Antigua, **Fridas** (3a Avenida 14-60 Zona 10, tel. 2367-1611/13, lunch and dinner daily) serves Mexican dishes that include tasty fajitas and flautas at fairly reasonable prices ($5-10). The chicken in mango sauce is delectable, and the bar makes excellent margaritas. Pick your poison from the long list of tequilas ($4-12). The most casual of all the Mexican food options is **Ta'contento** (14 Calle 1-42 Zona 10, tel. 2444-4080, www.tacontento. com, 11am-midnight Tues.-Sun., $3-7), where you can eat tasty tacos alfresco fronting a lively Zona Viva street.

FRENCH

There has always been considerable French influence on Guatemalan culture, which is also evident in the city's culinary offerings. Among the excellent options are **Saint-Honoré** (14 Calle 2-51 Zona 10, tel. 2379-4548, 11:30am-11pm daily), inside the InterContinental hotel, a typical French bakery serving cakes and some of Guatemala's best coffee. Also in the hotel lobby is the excellent **Café de la Paix** (6am-11pm daily), the only franchise of the famous Parisian brasserie chain outside of France, serving heavier meals, including entrecôte and onion soup ($12-25).

★ **Jean Francois** (Diagonal 6, 13-63 Zona 10, tel. 2333-4785, www.grupoculinario. com, noon-3pm and 7pm-10:30pm Mon.-Fri., noon-3pm Sat., $8-25) is a longtime favorite with Guatemala's wealthy elite and arguably one of the finest restaurants in Latin America. The atmosphere is elegant with tablecloths and flowers adorning the tables and antique colonial furniture in the lounge. Entrées include snook in a cream and lemon sauce with fine herbs and steak *bondelaise* with porcini mushrooms. Try the fantastic cold lemon soufflé with caramel sauce for dessert.

A more casual and yet very tasty French dining option is **Enchanté** (20 Calle 25-96 Zona 10, Centro Comercial La Plaza, Local 15A, tel. 2366-9000). With pleasant indoor and outdoor seating at Plaza Fontabella, ★ **Clio's** (4a Avenida 12-59 Zona 10, tel. 2336-6949, www.cliosbistro.com, 12:30pm-3:30pm and 6:30pm-10:30pm Mon.-Sat., 12:30pm-3:30pm Sun., $25) serves classic French cuisine in a tasteful atmosphere with excellent service.

GUATEMALAN

For gourmet Guatemalan cuisine served in a wonderful atmosphere accented by a high-roofed thatch ceiling, head to ★ **Kacao** (2a Avenida between 13 and 14 Calle, Zona 10,

Señora Pu at work in her kitchen

tel. 2337-4188/89, www.kacao.com.gt, lunch and dinner daily, $7-13). You can try a variety of traditional Guatemalan dishes, including spicy beef and chicken dishes in *pepián* and *jocón* sauces as well as corn-based delicacies such as *chuchitos* and tamales. In the downtown area, another popular place for Guatemalan cuisine is Arrin Cuan (5a Avenida 3-27 Zona 1, tel. 2238-0242, or 5a Avenida 10-22 Zona 9, tel. 2366-2660, www.arrincuan.com, 7am-10pm daily, $5-10), with many dishes from the Cobán region, including *kakik* stew, but also some less adventurous recipes such as chicken in apple sauce. The atmosphere is charmingly simple. Another good place for hearty Guatemalan fare is Casa Chapina (1a Avenida 13-42 Zona 10, tel. 2367-6688 or 2368-0663, www.restaurantecasachapina.com, lunch and dinner daily, $8-20), serving well-presented Guatemalan dishes such as *pollo en salsa de loroco* accompanied by fresh avocado and corn on the cob. An awesome new discovery is ★ La Cocina de la Señora Pu (6a Avenida "A" 10-16 Zona 1, tel. 5055-6480, www.senorapu.com, lunch daily, $7-15), where you'll find a modern take on traditional Mayan fare. Señora Pu hails from Quiché department, and you can watch her lovingly prepare dishes before your very eyes in the cozy open-air kitchen. There are beef, lamb, pork, chicken, and even duck dishes cooked in a variety of traditional sauces. You can wash it all down with traditional cacao-based beverages.

ASIAN

Sushi places seem to have sprung up all over town recently—even the Holiday Inn and Radisson each have their own sushi restaurants in their respective lobbies. The best of the hotel lobby sushi places, however, is ★ Tanoshii (14 Calle 2-51 Zona 10, tel. 2379-4548, noon-3pm and 6:30pm-11pm Mon.-Sat., $10-25), inside the InterContinental hotel, also serving Japanese dishes in a hip, ultramodern setting. Also in Zona 10 is Sushi Itto (4a Avenida 16-01 Zona 10, tel. 2366-7676, www.sushi-itto.com, lunch and dinner daily). The

city's best Thai restaurant, ★ Khawp Khun Kha (13 Calle A y 7a Ave. Zona 10, Centro Comercial Plaza Tiffany, tel. 2367-1719, noon-3pm and 7pm-10:30pm Tues.-Sat., $7-15) features tasty pad thai but also has a number of other great dishes such as chicken satay, beef in coffee sauce, and hearty soups.

For Chinese food, downtown there's Long Wah (6a Calle 3-75 Zona 1, tel. 2232-6611, lunch and dinner daily) with reasonably priced staple dishes you can eat in or take out. It's the best of several Chinese places west of the central plaza. China Town (13 Calle and Avenida La Reforma Zona 10, tel. 2331-9574, lunch and dinner Mon.-Sat.) delivers to the Zona 10 hotels, or you can enjoy your meal in its pleasant atmosphere.

AMERICAN

You'll find a number of familiar restaurant chains in Guatemala City, including Applebee's, T.G.I. Friday's, Chili's, IHOP, and Tony Roma's. For a local take on American fare, check out Frisco Grill (4a Avenida 12-59 Zona 10, Plaza Fontabella; tel. 2336-7147/48, www.friscogrill.com.gt, 11am-11:30pm Mon.-Sat., 7am-10pm Sun., $15). There's outdoor patio seating and tasty American favorites such as nachos, burgers, steak sandwiches, fish-and-chips, and quesadillas. I'm a big fan of their margaritas. One of only three in Central America, Hard Rock Café Guatemala City (1a Avenida y 13 Calle Zona 10, Edificio Dubai Center, tel. 2332-3862, www.hardrock.com/cafes/guatemala-city, noon-12:30am Mon.-Sat., 11am-10pm Sun., $10-25) serves the usual HRC fare including nachos, burgers, and decent sandwiches. A chainwide menu revamp has brought tasty fish and steak dishes to the menu, which you can enjoy amidst a backdrop of rock 'n' roll memorabilia and loud music. The Rock Shop, on the ground floor, sells destination-themed souvenirs and opens an hour earlier.

ITALIAN

Pecorino (11 Calle 3-36 Zona 10, tel. 2360-3035, www.ristorantepecorino.com, noon-1am Mon.-Sat., $12-30) is an excellent choice for its authentic Italian food, including brick-oven pizza, seafood dishes, steak, pasta, salads, and panini served in an attractive old-world atmosphere. There's also a huge wine selection. ★ **Enoteca Toscana** (20 calle 12-84 Zona 10, Plaza Ferco, tel. 4739-6393, $15-40) is an authentic Italian restaurant with mouthwatering dishes lovingly made by its chef-owner Leonardo Nardini. Many of the ingredients used are imported from Italy, which is reflected in the prices. Worth it, if you ask me. In a modern, casual setting with attractive blue-and-white-checkered tablecloths, **Tre Fratelli** (2a Avenida 13-25 Zona 10, tel. 2420-5350, www.trefratelli.com.gt, noon-1am daily) serves ample portions of very good food in a lively atmosphere with prices in the $5-10 range. It's part of a growing chain of restaurants with locations in the United States, Mexico, and Central America. Other Guatemala City locations can be found in Zona 11 and Carretera a El Salvador. I love the country atmosphere and cool decor at ★ **L'Osteria** (4a Avenida 10-41 Zona 10, tel. 2278-9914, www.saulemendez.com, noon-10pm Mon.-Thurs., noon-midnight Fri./Sat., noon-6pm Sun., $10-16). The menu is actually a mix of Italian, Mediterranean, and Greek food. There's indoor seating (with open windows) in the remains of an old, tin-roofed farmhouse or outside on a patio under the shade of a 100-year-old avocado tree. You'll get 15 percent off your check if you ride your bike here.

My favorite pizza place is **Margherita** (Boulevard Vista Hermosa 23-41 Zona 15, tel. 2375-0000, margherita.gt, lunch and dinner daily, $10-20). There's phenomenal brick-oven pizza prepared New York-style, thin crust, Neapolitan, or Sicilian. There are tasty salads, antipasti, and calzone that you can wash down with beer or wine. The atmosphere is modern and casual with indoor or outdoor seating and electronica music on the stereo. You can dine in or carry out. Another good option for brick-oven pizza served in a casual atmosphere is **Pizzeria Vesuvio** (18 Calle 3-36 Zona 10 and three other locations, tel. 2323-2323, www.vesuvio.com.gt, lunch and dinner daily, $7-15). A trusted reader and in-the-know Guatemala City resident recommends **L'Apero** (Vía 5 2-24, Local 5, Zona 4, tel. 2360-2561, noon-3pm Mon.-Tues., noon-3pm and 6pm-10pm Wed.-Fri., noon-10pm Sat., $5-12), where there's tasty pizzas in an assortment of uncommon flavors. Try the scrumptious blue cheese and pear pizza.

colorful decor of L'Osteria

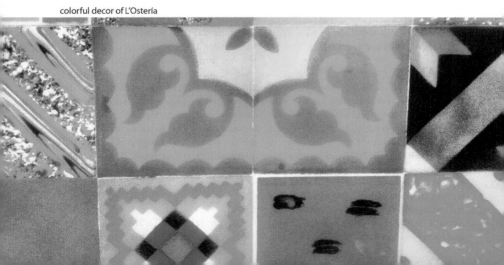

FUSION CUISINE AND FINE DINING

Many Guatemalan chefs study overseas early in their careers, which is clearly evident in the international influence permeating the city's excellent fusion cuisine. In other cases, talented chefs from New York and other international cities have set up shop in Guatemala, completely raising the bar for everyone else. Such is the case of ★ Jake's (17 Calle 10-40 Zona 10, tel. 2368-0351, www.restaurantejakes.com, noon-3pm and 7pm-10:30pm Mon.-Sat., noon-4pm Sun., $10-25), started by New York City artist-turned-chef Jake Denburg. Several unique features come together to make a visit to Jake's something truly special. For one, it has a wonderful atmosphere in a converted house with tile floors and wooden ceilings, interesting photography, and tables covered in butcher paper (crayons supplied). But nothing tops the eclectic menu and exquisite food. The wine list is also impressive, and rounding out your meal with one of the delectable homemade cheesecakes is a must.

A wonderful new addition to the city's already impressive list of restaurants is **Gracia, Cocina de Autor** (corner of 14 Calle and 4a Avenida Zona 10, tel. 2366-8699, noon-11pm Tues.-Sun., $8-20). Chef Pablo Novales has lived and worked in Spain, Switzerland, France, and England, gaining considerable culinary prowess evident in the dishes on the menu. The atmosphere is cozy, modern, and casual, with a small outdoor lounge next to the bar. I like the porcini mushroom risotto and Asian tuna avocado salad for starters, and the chicken kebabs in sesame seed sauce for the main course. The refreshing papaya sangria is a great way to get things started.

Also serving as a culinary school, **Camille** (9a Avenida 15-27 Zona 10, tel. 2368-0048 or 2367-1525, noon-3pm and 7pm-10pm Tues.-Fri., 7pm-10pm Sat., $10-15) serves creatively prepared fish, chicken, and seafood dishes. The steak in chipotle sauce served on a cheese *pupusa* (Salvadoran cheese-filled tortilla) is truly extraordinary. The atmosphere is pleasantly cozy with carbon sketches etched on the white plaster walls and also on ripped-out pages from spiral-bound notebooks framed and hung.

A longtime favorite is ★ **Tamarindos** (11 Calle 2-19A Zona 10, tel. 2360-5630, tamarindos.com.gt/en, noon-3pm and 7pm-10:30pm Mon.-Sat., 11am-3pm Sat. brunch; bar open 6pm-1am Mon.-Sat., $10-20), which makes some fine sushi and does an excellent job of

Tamarindos Bistro

combining Thai, Italian, and Guatemalan flavors into some irresistible dishes. There is pleasant indoor and outdoor garden patio seating and the hip ambience is set by postmodern decor and electronica music on the stereo. Try the crab-and-almond-stuffed mushrooms or the four-cheese gnocchi as an appetizer. The snook in banana sauce makes a fine main course. A spin-off of Tamarindos in a more casual environment is **Tamarindos Bistro** (Plaza Majadas ONCE, Zona 11, tel. 2473-7528, www.bistro.tamarindos.com.gt, 7am-10pm Mon.-Sat., 7am-8pm Sun., $8-20). There's a varied menu that includes delicious breakfasts, sushi, tasty sandwiches (try the Philly cheesesteak), and seafood.

Zona 14 also has some highly recommended restaurants. Amid spacious gardens is ★ **Ambia** (10a Avenida 5-49 Zona 14, tel. 2312-4690, www.fdg.com.gt, noon-midnight Mon.-Sat., $13-50), where the emphasis is on New Age cuisine consisting largely of Asian recipes, including Thai chicken and shrimp recipes, tuna tartare, flavorful soups, Italian pastas, and even gourmet burgers. There are decadent desserts, including black-and-white chocolate mousse and pears in red wine. The wine list, incidentally, is extensive and includes several fine malbecs and even a $700 bottle of Chilean Errazuriz Viñedo Chadwick Cabernet Sauvignon.

In the suburbs just east of the city, ★ **Tua** (Km. 14.5 Carretera a El Salvador, Centro Comercial Escala, tel. 6637-5443 or 6646-7038, $30) is a bistro serving wonderful cuisine that is on par with the fabulous volcano views off in the distance. It's definitely a place to choose outside seating, but the inside is modern and attractive as well, with dramatic high ceilings. I like the tuna tataki and coconut-breaded shrimp. The lamb chops and chipotle chicken are also fabulous.

In the city center and recommended more for the historical atmosphere than the somewhat overpriced, uninspired food is **Casa del Callejon Castillo Hermanos** (2a Ave. "A" 13-20 Zona 1, tel. 2366-5671, $15-35). Set in an old colonial home brimming with charm, the museum-like locale documents the life and times of the city's wealthy Castillo family, of Gallo beer fame. Interspersed with elegant dining areas are old photos, family heirlooms, and cool antique furniture on display. It makes a perfectly good place for a drink in a fancy, old-fashioned atmosphere. The best nights to visit are those featuring special performances of live jazz and tango, as dinner is often included in the admission price and tends to include better fare.

SEAFOOD
Donde Mikel (6a Ave. 13-32 Zona 10, tel. 2363-3308, lunch and dinner Mon.-Fri., lunch Sat.) serves some of the city's best seafood and grilled steak in a casual atmosphere. Its surf-and-turf plates are a popular favorite.

Information and Services

TOURIST INFORMATION
The main office of the **Guatemala Tourist Commission (INGUAT)** is at 7a Avenida 1-17 Zona 4, and it is open 8am-4pm Monday-Friday. Your best bet, however, is to stop by its kiosk in the airport arrivals area, which is open 6am-9pm. It also has smaller offices inside the **Palacio Nacional de la Cultura** (Parque Central, tel. 2253-0748), which keeps odd hours, and the historic **Palacio de** Correos (Main Post Office, 7a Avenida 11-67 Zona 1, tel. 2251-1898, 9am-5pm Mon.-Fri.).

MAPS
The best maps of Guatemala are *Mapas de Guatemala* (tel. 2232-1850, www.mapasdeguatemala.com), a series of beautifully illustrated, full-color maps of Guatemala's main tourist regions that also include helpful information on local businesses. The free

Staying Safe in Guatemala City

Guatemala City can be a dodgy place, though some *zonas* are certainly more prone to crime than others. Most of the areas frequented by tourists are relatively safe, though the downtown area (Zona 1) is by far the country's purse-snatching and pickpocketing hub. Exercise common sense and caution when in public areas. Never leave valuables in a parked car and avoid flashing expensive items such as laptops and cell phones in public places.

Pay careful attention when using ATMs. Some thieves have been so ingenious as to set up fake keypads at the entrance to ATM kiosks asking cardholders to enter their PIN numbers in order to gain access to the machine. You should never enter your PIN number anywhere other than on the ATM keypad itself.

Riding public buses is not usually a good idea, though the new transit system, the Transmetro, has proven much safer. If driving, it's a good idea to keep the car doors locked and the windows rolled all the way up. (Make sure your car's air-conditioning system is working properly so as to avoid the temptation to roll down the windows when it gets hot out.) Avoid talking on a cell phone while driving; it will keep you alert to your surroundings and will not draw undue attention from potential thieves. Cell phones are a favorite target, as is flashy jewelry. Recently, some parts of the city have become prone to robberies whereby the perpetrators (usually on motorcycles) target cars stopped at traffic lights. In most cases, the victims have been talking on their cell phones or are women traveling alone and wearing expensive jewelry. For this reason, many Guatemalans tint their windows to keep prying eyes away from the contents of their car. If you are the victim of a robbery or witness one, dial 120 from any phone.

Watch out for a common scam, particularly in the vicinity of the airport, whereby a "Good Samaritan" informs you of a flat tire on your car. If you can confirm that you indeed have a flat, pull over in a well-lit, public place. Do not stop at the side of the road to change the tire. If you are able to make it to a public place such as a gas station, have someone in your party stay inside the car or keep an eye on it yourself while you a gas station attendant changes the tire for you. The important thing is not to lose sight of the inside of your vehicle for a moment. Thieves can be extremely crafty at distracting you and getting into your car; locked doors may be a deterrent but will not stop thieves if they've already targeted you. For information on other precautions and common scams while traveling in Guatemala, see the State Department's Consular Information Sheet online at http://travel.state.gov.

In November 2008, the U.S. Embassy issued safety warnings for certain Guatemalan roads. Among the areas mentioned was the road east of kilometer 13 of Carretera a El Salvador. Due to its popularity with the city's wealthy residents, it appears this sector has become the scene of several violent robberies, carjackings, and kidnappings. The embassy recommends avoiding travel beyond kilometer 13 between 9pm and 6am. The document also recommends avoiding travel on the following roads outside Guatemala City: Routes 4 and 11 in the vicinity of Lake Atitlán and Route 14 between Antigua and Escuintla.

For this and other pertinent information, visit http://guatemala.usembassy.gov.

maps are available at INGUAT and at tourist gift shops and restaurants seemingly everywhere. You can also find interactive versions on their website. **ITMB Publishing** (530 W. Broadway, Vancouver, BC, Canada, 604/879-3621, www.itmb.com) publishes an excellent *International Travel Map of Guatemala* ($10.95), which is weatherproof and can be found at well-known bookstores in the United States.

COMMUNICATIONS

The **main post office** (8:30am-5pm Mon.-Fri., 8:30am-1pm Sat.) is downtown at 7a Avenida 11-67 Zona 1. There are also branches at the airport and the corner of Avenida La Reforma and 14 Calle Zona 9 with the same hours. It's called El Correo. Now you can find post office locations and even track packages online via their website at www.elcorreo.com.gt.

For faster service, many people prefer to use one of the international couriers, including FedEx (14 Calle 3-51 Zona 10, Edificio Murano Center Local No. 1, tel. toll-free from Guatemala 1-801-00-333-39, www.fedex.com. gt), UPS (5a Avenida 7-92 Zona 14, Local 4, CC Euroshops, tel. 2421-6000, www.ups. com), and DHL (12 Calle 5-12 Zona 10, tel. 2332-7547, www.dhl.com). For an all-in-one shipping locale, try Fast Mail (5a Avenida 7-42 Zona 14, tel. 2246-4646, www.fastmail-center.com, 8:30am-5:30pm Mon.-Fri., 9am-1pm Sat.).

MONEY

You can exchange dollars and cash travelers checks at virtually all of the city's banks. ATMs linked to international networks can be found all over the city. Be especially careful when withdrawing money at ATMs in the downtown area. The safest places to hit up an ATM are the Guatemala City shopping malls and hotel lobbies. There are money exchange kiosks at La Aurora International Airport, though you'll get much better rates elsewhere.

You can search for Visa ATM locations online at www.visa.com/atmlocator and MasterCard ATMs at www.mastercard.com/atm. A useful listing of Banco Industrial Visa ATM machines throughout Guatemala can be found at www.bi.com.gt.

The American Express agent in Guatemala City is Clark Tours (7a Avenida 14-76, Plaza Clark, Zona 9, tel. 2412-4700, www.clarktours. com). It also has offices in the Westin Camino Real and Barceló hotels.

LAUNDRY

Downtown there's Lavandería El Siglo (12 Calle 3-42 Zona 1, tel. 2230-0223, www. lavanderiaelsiglo.com, 8am-6pm Mon.-Fri., 8am-3pm Sat., $4 per load). There are other locations throughout the city. In Zona 10 is Lavandería Obelisco (20 Calle 2-16 Zona 10, tel. 2368-1469), where self-service laundry costs about $3 per load to wash and dry.

MEDICAL SERVICES

Guatemala City is becoming a destination for medical tourism, with many excellent private hospitals. Public clinics such as the Clínica Cruz Roja (Red Cross Clinic, 3a Calle 8-40 Zona 1, 8am-5:30pm Mon.-Fri., 8am-noon Sat.) offer free or low-cost consultations. Private clinics with doctors who speak English include the highly recommended 24-hour Hospital Centro Medico (6a Avenida 3-47 Zona 10, tel. 2279-4949, www.centromedico. com.gt) and the Hospital Herrera Llerandi (6a Avenida 8-71 Zona 10, tel. 2384-5959 or 2334-5955 emergencies, www.herrerallerandi. com). Grupo Hospitalario Guatemala (www.hospitalesdeguatemala.com) also has a good network of hospitals in the Guatemala City metro area.

EMERGENCY

Dial 120 from any phone for the police (6a Avenida and 14 Calle Zona 1). For emergency medical assistance, dial 125 for the Red Cross. For the fire department, dial 122 or 123.

IMMIGRATION

The offices of Migración (tel. 2361-8476, www.migracion.gob.gt) are on the second floor of the INGUAT building at 7a Avenida 1-17 Zona 4 and are open 8am-2:45pm Monday-Friday.

TRAVEL AGENTS

For booking plane tickets and onward travel within Guatemala, a good choice is Viajes Tivoli (6a Avenida 8-41 Zona 9, tel. 2386-4200, or 12 Calle 4-55 Zona 1, Edificio Herrera, tel. 2298-1050, www.tivoli.com.gt), as is Clark Tours (7a Avenida 14-76, Plaza Clark, Zona 9, tel. 2412-4700, www.clarktours.com). Clark Tours also has offices in the Westin Camino Real, Holiday Inn, and Barceló.

Transportation

GETTING THERE
Air

The once-wonky **La Aurora International Airport** (GUA, www.dgac.gob.gt), in Zona 13 six kilometers south of the city center, underwent a major expansion and renovation in 2007 and is now one of Central America's largest and most modern airports. Services include a bank, ATMs, various restaurants, excellent duty-free shopping, souvenir shops, and a post office. Members of United Airlines' United Club enjoy access to the airport's Copa Club, a lounge operated jointly with Copa Airlines and located next to gate 14. It's also open to First Class passengers traveling on United, Copa, or Star Alliance partners. Not traveling in first class? You can pay a day fee to visit ($50) if traveling on any of these airlines. Guests enjoy a TV lounge, free cocktails, wireless Internet, and space to relax before the flight.

Immigration, customs, and baggage claim are on the main building's first floor, while departures and check-in counters are on the third floor. There are technically two adjacent terminals, though they are merged into one large facility. The first area, known as *finger central,* consists of six gates for widebody aircraft. It fronts the main terminal, which is all that remains of the original facility dating to the 1960s. The second terminal, known as *finger norte,* consists of gates 7 to 19 and is seamlessly integrated into the rest of the terminal building. There is a food court on the fourth floor of the main terminal building overlooking the check-in counters. Additional restaurants can be found past the security checkpoints leading to the two *fingers,* one floor down from the check-in lobby.

Immigration and customs procedures at La Aurora Airport are very straightforward. Customs (known as SAT) will look at your declaration paperwork (to be filled out on the airplane prior to arrival) and will either put you in a line where your bags will be searched and applicable duties (if any) collected or will simply wave you on. Most foreign travelers are waved on, as what they're mostly looking for are arriving Guatemalans with loot from stateside shopping sprees. A disproportionate number of bags per traveler are usually a sure tip-off.

Guatemala City's underutilized La Aurora International Airport

Taxis are easily booked from a kiosk inside the airport terminal, as are rental cars. A taxi from the airport costs $8-20 depending on what part of town you're going to. Avis, Budget, Hertz, and National have kiosks inside the airport terminal. Their lots are across the road fronting the airport's three-level parking garage. If you're arriving on a later flight and have never driven Guatemala City's chaotic streets before, it might make more sense to take advantage of free airport shuttles to Zona 10 hotels and have the rental car company drop off the vehicle at your hotel the next morning. You could also just as easily take a cab or shuttle from your hotel to the airport the following day and pick up the car at that time.

If most of your travel involves the Guatemala City and Antigua area, my advice is to forgo a car rental in favor of taxis and shuttle buses. You can also hire a driver to take you around for about US$75-100 a day. Local hotel concierges can usually recommend someone for you. Doing so will allow you to get a feel for the city without the stress of having to drive on its unfamiliar streets. It will also allow you to get acquainted with the particular style of Guatemalan urban driving you'll need to adopt if you do end up driving here.

If you're bypassing Guatemala City altogether, you'll find shuttle vans to Antigua (about $20) are easily booked upon arrival at the airport. There is also a very helpful INGUAT (Instituto Guatemalteco de Turismo) information desk just after passing customs. It's staffed by English-speaking agents who can help you get your bearings.

It's not a good idea to ride a public bus into the city, especially at night. The Transmetro is perfectly safe and efficient, but its coverage area is limited. It will not get you to or from the airport, though the newer *eje central* route can get you as close as Bulevar Liberacion, which fronts the airport runway's northern extreme.

Several U.S. and foreign carriers fly daily into Guatemala City. Most of these airlines have city ticket offices, including **American Airlines** (Barceló Guatemala City, 7a Avenida 15-45 Zona 9, tel. 2422-0000), **United Airlines** (18 Calle 5-56, Edificio Unicentro, Local 704, Zona 10, tel. 2385-9610 or 801/812-6684 toll-free), **Delta** (15 Calle 3-20 Zona 10, Centro Ejecutivo, Primer Nivel, tel. 2337-0642), **Avianca** (Avenida Hincapié 12-22, Zona 13, tel. 2470-8222), and **Iberia** (Avenida La Reforma 8-60 Zona 9, tel. 2332-0911). American Airlines and United Airlines passengers can check bags in the day before their flight at service centers in the Barceló Guatemala City hotel (7a Avenida 15-45 Zona 9).

The only **domestic service** is to Flores, near the ruins of Tikal, though other routes may open if government plans to revamp several smaller airports throughout the country ever come to fruition. The only airline leaving from the main terminal for domestic flights is Avianca, with several daily flights to Flores. Local carrier **TAG** (Ave. Hincapie y 18 Calle Zona 13, tel. 2380-9494, www.tag.com.gt) offers service from the other side of the runway at its private hangar.

The airport is located 6 km south of downtown Guatemala City and 25 km from Antigua.

Bus

Guatemala City's unattractive Zona 4 bus terminal is being phased out (at least in part) thanks to a long-overdue plan to bring order to the chaos traditionally characterizing the state of public transportation, both within and into and out of the city. Accounting for 80 percent of the bedlam are buses arriving from and departing to the Western Highlands and the Pacific Coast. Buses to and from both of these regions were to be based out of the **Central de Transferencias Sur (CENTRA Sur)** in Zona 12, on the southern outskirts of the city, though this was only partly implemented. From CENTRA Sur, a series of modern, bright green interconnected buses known as *buses articulados* take passengers on a new system called the **Transmetro** into the city center. **CENTRA Norte** (CA-9 Norte 40-26 Zona 17, Km 8.5, tel. 2500-9800, www.centranorte.com.gt) was unveiled in 2012 and serves as the hub for buses heading out along the highway leading east to Izabal, Las Verapaces, and Petén. It's open 24/7 and has a modern shopping center with stores and restaurants. The city's public transportation system, meanwhile, is being replaced almost entirely by the Transmetro, a sort of surface metro, which will cover the entire metropolitan area by 2020 (or so they tell us).

A number of the (mostly) **first-class buses** heading to the Highlands and the Pacific Coast still leave from their own depots spread throughout the city, and this will probably continue to be the case for some time. The consolidation of bus routes heading east to Izabal, Las Verapaces, and Petén has been more successful. Here is the information on some of the more popular first-class bus routes:

To Chiquimula (3.5 hours, $4, 170 km): **Rutas Orientales** (CENTRA Norte, tel. 2503-3100, www.rutasorientales.com), departures every half hour 4:30am-6pm, or **Transportes Guerra** (CENTRA Norte), every half hour 7am-6pm.

To Cobán (4.5 hours, $5, 213 km): **Transportes Escobar Monja Blanca** (CENTRA Norte) has hourly buses 4am-5pm, stopping at El Rancho and the Quetzal Biotope.

To Esquipulas (4.5 hours, $5, 222 km): **Rutas Orientales** (CENTRA Norte, tel. 2503-3100, www.rutasorientales.com), has departures every half hour 4:30am-6pm.

To Flores (eight hours, $10-30 depending on service level, 500 km): Options include **Línea Dorada** (CENTRA Norte, tel. 2415-8900,www.lineadorada.com.gt), with luxury buses departing at 10am and 9pm ($30), or a more economical overnight bus leaving at 10pm ($16). **Fuente del Norte** (CENTRA Norte, tel. 2251-3817) has about 20 daily departures ($10-20).

To Huehuetenango (five hours, 266 km): **Los Halcones** (7a Avenida 15-27 Zona 1, tel. 2238-1929, $5), departs at 4am, 7am, 10:15am, 2pm, and 5pm. **Transportes Velásquez** (20 Calle 1-37 Zona 1, tel. 2221-1084, $4) has nine buses daily. **Transportes Zaculeu Futura** (9a Calle 11-42 Zona 1, tel. 2232-2858, $5), has buses at 6am and 3pm.

To La Mesilla (seven hours, $6, 345 km): **Transportes Velásquez** (20 Calle 1-37 Zona 1, tel. 2221-1084, $5.50), every two hours 5:30am-1:30pm.

To Panajachel (three hours, 148 km): **Transportes Rebuli** (21 Calle and 4a Avenida Zona 1, $2) has hourly buses 5:30am-3:30pm.

To Puerto Barrios (five hours, 295 km): **Litegua** (CENTRA Norte, tel. 2220-8840, www.litegua.com) has 16 buses daily 4:30am-7pm.

To Quetzaltenango (four hours, $4.50, 205 km): **Transportes Álamo** (21 Calle 0-14 Zona 1, tel. 2251-4838) has six buses a day 8am-5:30pm. **Líneas América** (2a Avenida 18-47 Zona 1, tel. 2232-1432) has seven buses a day 5am-7:30pm. **Transportes Galgos** (7a Avenida 19-44 Zona 1, tel. 2253-4868) leaves seven times daily 5:30am-7pm. The newest option is a nonstop bus on an ultraluxurious coach aboard **Línea Dorada** (16 Calle 10-03 Zona 1, tel. 2220-7900 or 2232-9658, www.lineadorada.com.gt, $6) at 8am and 3pm.

To Río Dulce (six hours, $6-21, 280 km): **Línea Dorada** (CENTRA Norte, tel. 2415-8900, www.lineadorada.com.gt) has luxury buses departing at 10am and 9pm ($21), or a more economical bus leaving at 10pm ($11). Both continue to Flores. **Litegua** (CENTRA Norte, tel. 2220-8840, www.litegua.com) has buses at 6am, 9am, 11:30am, and 1pm.

To Zacapa (three hours, $3.50): **Rutas Orientales** (CENTRA Norte, tel. 2503-3100, www.rutasorientales.com) has 15 buses daily.

International Bus

To Copán, Honduras (five hours, 238 km, $35): **Hedman Alas** (2a Avenida 8-73 Zona 10, tel. 2362-5072, 2362-5073, or 2362-5074, www.hedmanalas.com) departs daily at 5am and 9am.

To San Salvador, El Salvador (five hours, 240 km): **Melva Internacional** (3a Avenida 1-38 Zona 9, tel. 2331-0874, $15) departs hourly 5am-4pm, with more expensive *especiales* ($20) leaving at 6:45am, 9am, and 3pm. **Tica Bus** (Calzada Aguilar Batres 22-55 Zona 12, tel. 2473-1639, www.ticabus. com, $20) leaves at 1pm. **King Quality** (18 Avenida 1-96 Zona 15, tel. 2369-0404, $30) has luxury buses departing at 6:30am, 8am, 2pm, and 3:30pm. **Pullmantur** (1a Avenida 13-22 Zona 10, Holiday Inn, tel. 2367-4746, www. pullmantur.com, $30-46) offers the most luxurious service on this route with double-decker buses and a choice of fare classes, departing at 7am and 3pm daily with additional buses Fridays at noon and Sundays at 4pm.

To Tapachula, Mexico (seven hours, 290 km): **Transportes Galgos** (7a Avenida 19-44 Zona 1, tel. 2253-4868, $22) has departures at 7:30am and 2pm. **Línea Dorada** (16 Calle 10-55 Zona 1, tel. 2232-5506, www.lineado-rada.com.gt, $22) departs at 8am.

GETTING AROUND
Taxi
Getting around by taxi can be tricky, as there is really only one reliable taxicab company in the city and it requires you to call for a pickup if you wish to hire its services. **Taxis Amarillo Express** (tel. 2470-1515 or 1766, www.amarilloexpress.com) is also one of the only companies to use meters. Otherwise, the airport taxis and those at the Zona Viva hotels are generally reliable. It's not usually a good idea to hail a cab from the street, as some of these are gypsy cabs and robberies do sometimes occur. If you find a reliable cab driver, you can always ask for a business card and hire his services for the rest of your stay or ask him to refer you to another reputable driver.

Car Rental
Several car rental agencies operate out of the airport and nearby areas, including **Avis** (6a Calle 7-64 Zona 9, tel. 2324-9000 or 800/331-1212 U.S. toll-free, www.avis. com.gt), **Dollar** (Avenida La Reforma 8-33

Zona 10, tel. 2385-8728 or 800/800-4000 U.S. toll-free, www.dollar.com.gt), **Budget** (6a Avenida 11-24 Zona 9, tel. 2332-7744 or 800/472-3325 U.S. toll-free, www.budget. com), **Hertz** (7a Avenida 14-84 Zona 13, tel. 2314-4411 or 800/654-3001 U.S. toll-free, also with offices inside the Westin Camino Real, InterContinental, and Barceló, www.rent-autos.com.gt), **Alamo** (La Aurora Airport, tel. 2362-2701, www.alamoguatemala.com), and **Thrifty** (7a Avenida 14-28 Zona 13, Aeropuerto La Aurora, tel. 2379-8747 to 52, or 800/847-4389 U.S. toll-free, www.thrifty. com).

Public Buses
Guatemala City's chaotic public bus transportation is not recommended for international travelers, mainly for safety considerations, as armed robberies and purse snatchings are frequent. Buses are also particularly susceptible to the city's increasing gang-related violence, and drivers are often harassed and/or murdered for money by gang members.

Transmetro
A glimmer of hope for the city's mass transit system emerged in 2007 with the unveiling of the Transmetro, a completely revamped public transportation system, which should be in full operation by 2020. The first phase, including the first transfer center (in Zona 12) for buses coming in from other parts of Guatemala, is already up and running and a second branch was scheduled to go into service at time of publication. Bus service via long, train-like interconnected green units brings travelers from the transfer center to the downtown area. More transfer centers are in the works.

The system promises to provide Guatemalans (and foreign travelers) with a safe, comfortable, and fast option for getting around the city. Buses stop at designated locations, drivers no longer trundle the streets competing for passengers, a prepaid system eliminates on-board cash, and buses and stations are guarded by cameras and plainclothes police officers. It

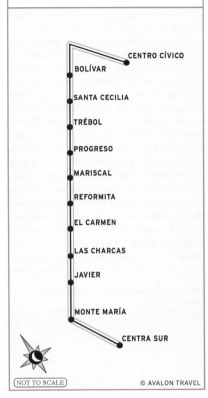

Transmetro Eje Centro Histórico

CENTRO CÍVICO
BOLÍVAR
SANTA CECILIA
TRÉBOL
PROGRESO
MARISCAL
REFORMITA
EL CARMEN
LAS CHARCAS
JAVIER
MONTE MARÍA
CENTRA SUR

NOT TO SCALE
© AVALON TRAVEL

Transmetro Eje Central

18 CALLE
EL CALVARIO
PLAZA BARRIOS
CENTRO CÍVICO
21 CALLE
9A AVENIDA
BANCO DE GUATEMALA
6A AVENIDA
7A AVENIDA
RUTA 3
4 GRADOS SUR
4 GARDOS NORTE
EXPOSICIÓN
RUTA 6
PLAZA DE LA REPÚBLICA
TERMINAL
TORRE DEL REFORMADOR
2A CALLE
INDUSTRIA SUR
SEIS 26
5A CALLE
IGSS ZONA 9
TIVOLI
12 CALLE
MONTÚFAR
PLAZA ESPAÑA
6A AVENIDA
7A AVENIDA
ACUEDUCTO
LOS ARCOS
BLVD LOS PROCERES

© AVALON TRAVEL
NOT TO SCALE

costs Q1 to ride the Transmetro and the system only accepts one-quetzal coins. Drop your coin in the slot, push past the turnstile, and wait for the next bus under a covered, raised platform.

For now, the Transmetro's routes include the *eje sur,* starting in Zona 12's CENTRA Sur and heading downtown to Zona 1's Plaza Amate, *corredor central,* and the newer *eje centro histórico.* The *eje sur* makes 12 stops along the way, including at the Centro Cívico (Plaza Municipal) and El Trébol. The *corredor central* route runs the length of 7a Avenida from Zona 1 to Zona 13's Avenida Las Américas all the way to Plaza Berlín, stopping at Zona 4's

bus terminal and Cuatro Grados Norte along the way. The bus terminal's status as the transportation hub for many bus lines will probably remain in place pending the gradual transition to the new system based on transfer centers. Direct Transmetro buses (no stops) heading from downtown to CENTRA leave from **Plaza Amate** (4a Avenida and 18 Calle Zona 1, 5am-9am and 4pm-9pm Mon.-Fri.). The *eje centro histórico* is quite convenient for visits to Guatemala's City's downtown sector, with a route that parallels Paseo de la Sexta and leaves you just one block from the central plaza at Parque Centenario.

Near Guatemala City

South of the city along Calzada Aguilar Batres, the sprawl continues into the adjacent district of Villa Nueva, a suburban housing and industrial area that has been swallowed up by the larger city. From here, the Carretera al Pacífico, or Pacific Highway (CA-9) leads south to Escuintla and the Pacific Coast.

LAKE AMATITLÁN

Amatitlán lies 30 kilometers south of Guatemala City on the road to the Pacific Coast. The lake is in the process of being rescued from what would have been certain ecological death caused by wastewater from nearby industry and uncontrolled urban growth. A new sewage treatment plant now filters the filthy waters of the Río Villalobos, which once flooded untreated sewage into the lake. Trees have been replanted, and the lake is being pumped with oxygen and cleaned of plants in an effort to reverse its eutrophication. It's still not possible to swim in the lake's waters, though it may be some day.

Recreation

The public beach of **Las Ninfas** was being remodeled by tourism authorities to include boat docks (for sailboats and motorboats), new food stalls, walkways, and landscaping, but like so many other projects in Guatemala it was never finished. The long-closed **Teleférico** (Aerial Tram, 9am-5pm Fri.-Sun., $2 adults, $0.85 children) was reopened in 2006, in an attempt to kick off the rebirth of one of Guatemala City's oldest recreational enclaves. The funicular climbs 350 meters up a mountainside along a 1.5-kilometer route. There's a lookout point at the top of the mountain where you can get out, appreciate the view of the lake and Guatemala City, and grab a bite to eat at a small cafeteria serving snacks. The Teleférico was unfortunately not operational

at the time of writing, and it's anyone's guess if it will be resuscitated any time soon.

If you'd rather just soak your weary bones in the warm waters of some pleasant hot springs, you can do that at **Kawilal Hotel & Spa** at Baños Termales Santa Teresita (Avenida Puente de la Gloria, Riveras del Río Michatoya, tel. 6644-1000, www.santateresita.com.gt, 9am-5:30pm Mon.-Thurs., 9am-7:30pm Fri., 8:30am-8:30pm Sat., 8:30am-6:30pm Sun. and holidays), where you can enjoy a private steam bath or a soak in a private tub filled with steaming hot water to your taste ($5). Several outdoor pools of varying temperatures are also available, and there's a restaurant serving grilled meats and chicken, salads, sandwiches, and seafood. Rounding out the list of offerings is a spa, where you can enjoy a one-hour massage for about $20. A modern, 18-room hotel (www.

aerial view of Lake Amatitlán, on the fringes of Guatemala City

kawilalhotel.com, $90 d) opened in 2013, with comfortable accommodations and its own swimming pool, restaurant, and bar.

Parque Nacional Naciones Unidas

This 491-hectare park near the lakeshore is managed by private conservation group **Defensores de la Naturaleza** (tel. 5651-4825 or 2310-2929, www.defensores.org.gt) and is open 8am-4pm Monday-Friday and 8am-5pm Saturday and Sunday. Admission is $3.50. Facilities include picnic areas with barbecue pits, hiking and mountain biking trails with hanging bridges and lookout points over the lake, basketball courts, and soccer fields. A five-platform, 400-meter canopy tour, and rappelling were added in 2008. There are miniature replicas of Guatemalan landmarks such as Tikal's Gran Jaguar temple and Antigua Guatemala in areas denominated "Plaza Guatemala" and "Plaza Antigua." The park is one of five original national parks dating back to 1955.

Getting There

You'll probably need to rent a car to get to Lake Amatitlán, though you could also hire a cab to take you there from Guatemala City for about $30. If you're driving, take the Pacific Highway (CA-9) south out of the city. The main entrance to the Amatitlán lakeshore is at Km. 26. You'll see signs. The exit veers off from the right side of the highway. From the exit ramp, you'll come to a Shell gas station, at which you turn left. Follow the road until it dead-ends just past the soccer fields on your left. Turn left at the dead end. You'll pass a bridge over the Río Michatoya on your right. The next left will take you to the Teleférico and farther up that same road is Parque Nacional Naciones Unidas. Turning right onto the bridge over the Río Michatoya followed by an immediate right will bring you to the Santa Teresita hot springs.

La Antigua Guatemala

Its name means "the old Guatemala," and this is in fact what it is. The former capital of Guatemala was destroyed by earthquakes in 1773. Rather than rebuild, the country's aristocracy opted for a fresh start in the neighboring Valley of the Hermitage, the current site of Guatemala City. And so, by decree, the city and its inhabitants moved on. Still, some Antigueños stayed behind, choosing to live among the ruins, coffee farms, verdant hillsides, and sentinel volcanoes. The city's colonial architecture was maintained, as there were no plans to rebuild, and its ruined churches and convents remained just that. It is said the remaining residents of Antigua were so poor that they had to subsist on avocados, earning them the nickname Panzas Verdes (Green Bellies).

Today, Antigua (as it is more commonly referred to) is a UNESCO World Heritage Site and home to much of Guatemala's expatriate population along with scores of international students studying in its many Spanish schools. Its brightly colored houses and cobblestone streets harbor some of Guatemala's finest restaurants, shopping, and art galleries in a fantastic mountain setting that has inspired artists, writers, and wanderers for centuries. Antigua is a pleasant mixture of Mayan and Spanish colonial influences and makes an excellent base from which to explore other parts of the country.

Antigua lies 45 kilometers from Guatemala City via a good, paved highway. Its setting is spectacular, flanked on its southern extreme by the towering 3,750-meter (12,325-foot) Agua Volcano. The colossal 4,235-meter (13,044-foot) Acatenango and active Fuego Volcanoes lie to the west. The surrounding hillsides provide wonderful views of the valley and the volcanoes, and are excellent terrain for recreational pursuits such as hiking and mountain biking. The climate is similar to that of Guatemala City, as Antigua lies at about the same altitude, just over 1,500 meters. Days are warm and nights are pleasantly cool.

Previous: view of Antigua from Cerro de la Cruz, with Agua Volcano in the background; a flower-strewn Antigua street. **Above:** one of Antigua's many ruined churches.

Highlights

★ **Parque Central:** You can't miss the town's central plaza, easily Guatemala's loveliest, and the heart and soul of Antigua (page 70).

★ **Arco de Santa Catalina:** A beautiful colonial archway, which is also one of Antigua's most photographed landmarks, provides a suitable frame for views of Agua Volcano (page 71).

★ **Cerro de la Cruz:** This large stone cross on a hill overlooking the valley and volcanoes makes for a good afternoon stroll. Bring a camera (page 72).

★ **Iglesia y Convento de las Capuchinas:** One of Antigua's best-preserved colonial monuments has many interesting features, including a tower and 18 nuns' cells built around a patio (page 72).

★ **Centro Cultural Casa Santo Domingo:** The city's finest museum lies on the grounds of a fantastic restored monastery, which now functions as a five-star hotel (page 73).

★ **Casa Popenoe:** This fully restored colonial mansion offers a rare glimpse into the life of a royal official in 17th-century Antigua in addition to wonderful city views from the second-story terrace (page 75).

★ **Finca El Zapote:** Lush botanical gardens lie just outside of Antigua, with jaw-dropping views of Fuego Volcano to boot (page 81).

★ **Volcano Climbs:** Antigua's fantastic mountain scenery is dominated by the presence of Agua, Fuego, and Acatenango Volcanoes, affording excellent opportunities for mountaineering at a variety of difficulty levels. Active Pacaya Volcano is another popular day trip (page 82).

★ **Centro Cultural La Azotea:** This three-in-one coffee, music, and indigenous costume museum has excellent displays and offers an interesting glimpse into many aspects of modern-day Mayan culture (page 102).

HISTORY

The former capital of Guatemala, now known as Ciudad Vieja, was the first of Guatemala's capitals to suffer merciless destruction at the hands of nature. It was built on the slopes of Agua Volcano; an earthquake on the evening of September 10, 1541, unleashed a torrent of mud and water that came tumbling down the volcano's slopes and destroyed the city. The new Muy Leal y Muy Noble Ciudad de Santiago de los Caballeros de Goathemala, as it would officially come to be known, was established on March 10, 1543, in the Panchoy Valley. The new capital would be no stranger to the ravages of nature; its first earthquake occurred only 20 years after the city's founding.

An earthquake in 1717 spurred an unprecedented building boom, with the city reaching its peak in the mid-18th century. At that time, its population would number around 60,000. Antigua was the capital of the Audiencia de Guatemala, under the jurisdiction of the larger Viceroyalty of New Spain, which encompassed most of present-day Mexico and all of Central America as far south as Costa Rica. The Viceroyalty's capital was in Mexico City, which along with Lima, Peru, would be the only other New World cities exceeding Antigua's political, cultural, and economic importance. Antigua boasted Central America's first printing press and one of the hemisphere's first universities and was known as an important center of arts and education. Among its outstanding citizens were conquistador and historian Bernal Díaz del Castillo, Franciscan friar and indigenous peoples rights advocate Bartolomé de las Casas, bishop Francisco Marroquín, artist Tomás de Merlo, English priest/traveler Thomas Gage, and architect Juan Bautista Antonelli.

Antigua's prominence came crashing down in 1773. The city was rocked throughout most of the year by a series of earthquakes, which later came to be known as the Terremotos de Santa Marta. Two earthquakes occurred on July 29. The final blows would be delivered on September 7 and December 13. The city was officially moved the following year to its present location in modern-day Guatemala City.

Antigua lay in ruins occupied mainly by squatters, its monuments pillaged for building materials for the new capital. It wasn't until the mid-19th century that it became once again populated and its buildings restored, in part with the money from the region's newfound coffee wealth. The city was declared a national monument in 1944 and came under the protection of the National Council for the Protection of Antigua Guatemala in 1969. It was declared a UNESCO World Heritage Site in 1979. The council has done a fairly decent job at protecting and restoring the city's cultural and architectural heritage, though building code violations are not at all unheard of. Still, many power lines have gone underground and truck traffic has been effectively banned from the city's streets, greatly reducing noise pollution.

PLANNING YOUR TIME

A week in Antigua would give you ample time to explore the town, its ruins, museums, and churches, maybe climb a volcano, visit a coffee farm, and do some shopping. Depending on whether or not you plan to study Spanish, you could easily spend several weeks in Antigua. Some choose to study Spanish for a week just to brush up on their skills or get a very basic foundation before moving on to other parts of Guatemala. At the minimum, you should plan on spending two nights here. Some have even recommended Antigua as a long weekend getaway from cities such as Miami, Atlanta, Houston, and Dallas because of its proximity and ease of access. The Guatemala City international airport is about a 45-minute drive away.

ORIENTATION

Getting around Antigua is fairly straightforward. True to its colonial foundations, it was laid out in a grid pattern surrounding the central plaza with *calles* running east-west and *avenidas* running north-south. The plaza is bounded by 4a Calle and 5a Calle to the north

La Antigua Guatemala

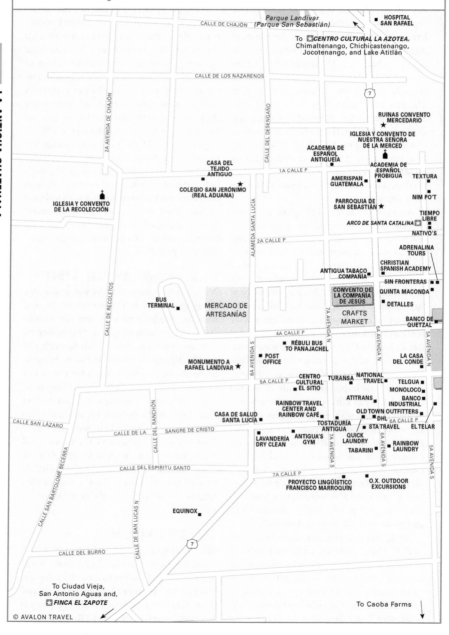

Parque Landívar
CALLE DE CHAJÓN   (Parque San Sebastián)

HOSPITAL SAN RAFAEL

To CENTRO CULTURAL LA AZOTEA,
Chimaltenango, Chichicastenango,
Jocotenango, and Lake Atitlán

CALLE DE LOS NAZARENOS

2A AVENIDA DE CHAJÓN

CALLE DEL DESENGAÑO

RUINAS CONVENTO
MERCEDARIO

IGLESIA Y CONVENTO DE
NUESTRA SEÑORA
DE LA MERCED

ACADEMIA DE
ESPAÑOL
ANTIGÜEÑA

ACADEMIA DE
ESPAÑOL
PROBIGUA

TEXTURA

CASA DEL
TEJIDO
ANTIGUO

1A CALLE P.

AMERISPAN
GUATEMALA

NIM PO'T

COLEGIO SAN JERÓNIMO
(REAL ADUANA)

ALAMEDA SANTA LUCÍA

PARROQUIA DE
SAN SEBASTIÁN

TIEMPO
LIBRE

IGLESIA Y CONVENTO
DE LA RECOLECCIÓN

ARCO DE SANTA CATALINA

NATIVO'S

2A CALLE P.

ADRENALINA
TOURS

CHRISTIAN
SPANISH ACADEMY

CALLE DE RECOLETOS

ANTIGUA TABACO
COMPAÑÍA

SIN FRONTERAS

QUINTA MACONDA

BUS
TERMINAL

MERCADO DE
ARTESANÍAS

CONVENTO DE
LA COMPAÑÍA
DE JESÚS

DETALLES

7A AVENIDA N

CRAFTS
MARKET

BANCO DE
QUETZAL

4A CALLE P.

6A AVENIDA N

5A AVENIDA N

8A AVENIDA S

RÉBULI BUS
TO PANAJACHEL

POST
OFFICE

LA CASA
DEL CONDE

MONUMENTO A
RAFAEL LANDÍVAR

CENTRO
CULTURAL
EL SITIO

TURANSA

NATIONAL
TRAVEL

TELGUA

5A CALLE P.

MONOLOCO

ATITRANS

BANCO
INDUSTRIAL

RAINBOW TRAVEL
CENTER AND
RAINBOW CAFÉ

OLD TOWN
OUTFITTERS

CASA DE SALUD
SANTA LUCÍA

DHL

6A CALLE P.

TOSTADURÍA
ANTIGUA

STA TRAVEL

EL TELAR

CALLE SAN LÁZARO

CALLE DE LA
SANGRE DE CRISTO

CALLE DEL RANCHÓN

LAVANDERÍA
DRY CLEAN

ANTIGUA'S
GYM

7A AVENIDA S

QUICK
LAUNDRY

6A AVENIDA S

RAINBOW
LAUNDRY

5A AVENIDA S

TABARINI

CALLE DEL ESPÍRITU SANTO

CALLE SAN BARTOLOMÉ BECERRA

7A CALLE P.

PROYECTO LINGÜÍSTICO
FRANCISCO MARROQUÍN

O.X. OUTDOOR
EXCURSIONS

CALLE DE SAN LUCAS N

EQUINOX

7

CALLE DEL BURRO

To Ciudad Vieja,
San Antonio Aguas and,
FINCA EL ZAPOTE

To Caoba Farms

© AVALON TRAVEL

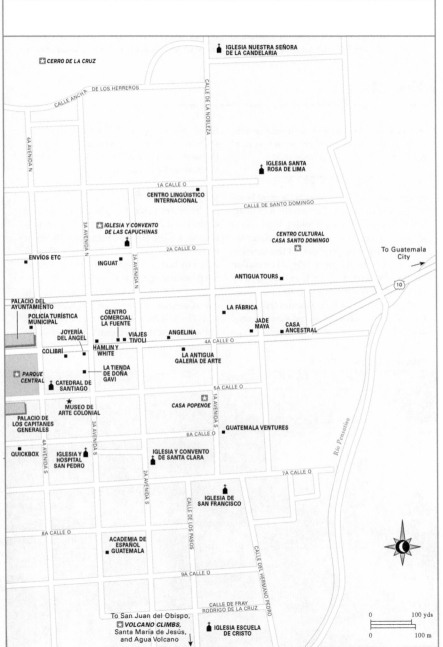

CERRO DE LA CRUZ

IGLESIA NUESTRA SEÑORA DE LA CANDELARIA

CALLE ANCHA DE LOS HERREROS

CALLE DE LA NOBLEZA

4A AVENIDA N

IGLESIA SANTA ROSA DE LIMA

1A CALLE O

CENTRO LINGÜÍSTICO INTERNACIONAL

CALLE DE SANTO DOMINGO

3A AVENIDA N

IGLESIA Y CONVENTO DE LAS CAPUCHINAS

CENTRO CULTURAL CASA SANTO DOMINGO

2A CALLE O

ENVÍOS ETC

INGUAT

2A AVENIDA N

ANTIGUA TOURS

To Guatemala City

10

PALACIO DEL AYUNTAMIENTO

POLICÍA TURÍSTICA MUNICIPAL

LA FÁBRICA

CENTRO COMERCIAL LA FUENTE

JADE MAYA

CASA ANCESTRAL

JOYERÍA DEL ANGEL

VIAJES TIVOLI

ANGELINA

4A CALLE O

COLIBRÍ

HAMLIN Y WHITE

LA ANTIGUA GALERÍA DE ARTE

LA TIENDA DE DOÑA GAVI

PARQUE CENTRAL

CATEDRAL DE SANTIAGO

5A CALLE O

MUSEO DE ARTE COLONIAL

CASA POPENOE

1A AVENIDA S

PALACIO DE LOS CAPITANES GENERALES

3A AVENIDA S

6A CALLE O

GUATEMALA VENTURES

Río Pensativo

QUICKBOX

4A AVENIDA S

IGLESIA Y HOSPITAL SAN PEDRO

IGLESIA Y CONVENTO DE SANTA CLARA

7A CALLE O

2A AVENIDA S

IGLESIA DE SAN FRANCISCO

CALLE DE LOS PASOS

8A CALLE O

ACADEMIA DE ESPAÑOL GUATEMALA

CALLE DEL HERMANO PEDRO

9A CALLE O

CALLE DE FRAY RODRIGO DE LA CRUZ

To San Juan del Obispo, VOLCANO CLIMBS, Santa María de Jesús, and Agua Volcano

IGLESIA ESCUELA DE CRISTO

0   100 yds

0   100 m

and south, and 4a Avenida and 5a Avenida to the east and west. Street addresses are labeled according to their direction relative to the plaza: Norte (North), Oriente (East), Sur (South), and Poniente (West). Most streets are known by this method, though all have names dating to colonial times. Only a handful of streets are known solely in this manner.

Sights

Antigua is fascinating and easily manageable, as most everything you might want to see and do lies within a radius of a few miles.

★ PARQUE CENTRAL

Antigua's central plaza is easily the most beautiful in the country and forms the hub of activity for shoe shiners, strolling lovers, tour groups, ice cream vendors, and foreign visitors. Gracing the central part of the square is a lovely fountain dating to 1936, a re-creation of an earlier version from 1738 destroyed by earthquakes. It is bordered by the Catedral de Santiago, Palacio de los Capitanes Generales, Palacio del Ayuntamiento, and a commercial arcade known as the Portal del Comercio. The *parque* makes a great place for a stroll or people-watching from its park benches. At night, the surrounding buildings and monuments are beautifully illuminated.

Catedral de Santiago

On its eastern side, the plaza is dominated by the beautiful **Catedral de Santiago** (entrance 5a Calle Oriente, 9am-5pm, $0.50). It was once wonderfully lit up at night, though currently half of the lightbulbs are out and one is left wondering when, if ever, they will be replaced. Its history, as is much of Antigua's, is one of constant destruction and reconstruction. The first cathedral built on this site dates to 1545, but its shoddy construction caused its

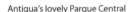

Antigua's lovely Parque Central

roof to come crashing down during an earthquake in 1583. It was decided to build a new cathedral in 1670, a task that would require 11 years and the conscripted labor of indigenous Maya. The scale of the new structure was astounding, with 18 chapels, a huge dome, five naves, and a large central chamber measuring 90 meters by 20 meters. It was graced by paintings and artwork of renowned European and colonial artists; its altar was inlaid with silver, ivory, and mother-of-pearl. Although it withstood the earthquakes of 1689 and 1717, it finally succumbed to the earthquakes of 1773.

The current church is not really a cathedral in the strict sense of the word, as it consists of two restored chambers known as the Parroquia de San José. You can visit the interesting interior, where you'll find splendid arches and towering columns. There is also a sculpted black Christ similar to the highly revered statue found in Esquipulas, both carved by Quirio Cataño. The remains of the rest of the colonial structure can also be seen here, a moss-covered mass of stones and rotting beams. The remains of some of the major players from colonial days are said to be buried beneath the church altar, including Don Pedro de Alvarado; his wife, Beatriz de la Cueva; Guatemala's first bishop, Francisco Marroquín; and conqueror/chronicler Bernal Díaz del Castillo. Steps behind the main altar lead to the former crypt, now a chapel, harboring the black Christ statue.

Palacio del Ayuntamiento

Found on the north side of the plaza, this large structure functioned as the town hall, also known as the Casa del Cabildo. It has miraculously withstood the test of time, resisting damage from earthquakes until the most recent one in 1976, despite its construction dating to 1740. Some fantastic views of the cathedral and Agua Volcano are framed by the Palacio del Ayuntamiento's beautiful arches from its second-floor balconies. Perhaps a bigger draw than the historical building itself is the quite interesting colonial fountain embossed with the emblem of

Santiago (St. James), found in a quiet courtyard. Next door, the Museo del Libro Antiguo (Antique Book Museum, tel. 7832-5511, 9am-4pm Tues.-Fri., 9am-noon and 2pm-4pm Sat.-Sun., $1.50) features exhibits on colonial printing and binding processes. There's a replica of the country's first printing press, brought to Guatemala in 1660 from Puebla, Mexico.

Palacio de los Capitanes Generales

On the south end of the plaza, the Palacio de los Capitanes Generales or Palace of the Captains General dates to 1558 and was once the seat of government for the entire Central American territory from Chiapas to Costa Rica, of which Antigua was the capital, until 1773. Its imposing architecture is dominated by a row of 27 arches on both of its floors. It once housed colonial rulers, the royal mint, the judiciary, and tax offices, among other things. It has been recently restored and now houses a cultural center, after much debate about what its function would be. Among the attractions is Museo de Armas de Santiago (tel. 7832-2878, 9am-5pm Tues.-Sun., $4). It houses colonial artifacts, weapons (including cannons), historical paintings, and furnishings.

★ ARCO DE SANTA CATALINA

Three blocks north of the park along 5a Avenida Norte (also known as Calle del Arco) is one of Antigua's most recognizable landmarks, the Arco de Santa Catalina. The Santa Catalina archway is all that remains of a convent dating to 1613. As the convent grew, it expanded to include a structure across the street. The arch then was built to allow the nuns to cross to the other side while avoiding contact with the general populace in accordance with strict rules governing seclusion. Its current version with a clock tower is a reconstruction dating to the 19th century, as the original was destroyed in the 1773 earthquakes. The clock is a French model, which needed to be wound every three days. It stopped working after the 1976 earthquake but was repaired in 1991. Looking south through the archway, you'll find some nice framing for an unobstructed view of Agua Volcano. The archway is practically an Antigua icon and beautifully painted in a rich orange hue with white accents that have become delightfully aged.

★ CERRO DE LA CRUZ

In the hills north of the city stands this giant stone cross, from which there are sweeping views south over the city with Agua Volcano in the background. Robberies were once frequent here until the creation of the tourism police, which began escorting visitors to the site and pretty much put an end to these crimes. It's still a good idea to go along with a police escort and to visit during daylight hours. Escorts are available free from the tourism police near the central plaza. You'll want to bring along your camera and some water. It's about a 30-minute walk from the plaza to the Cerro de la Cruz. From the top of the hill, you can see the entire Antigua Valley and the cross makes for a nice foreground element.

CHURCHES AND MONASTERIES
★ Iglesia y Convento de las Capuchinas

The Iglesia y Convento de las Capuchinas (2a Avenida Norte and 2a Calle Oriente, 9am-5pm daily, $4) was abandoned after being destroyed in the earthquakes of 1773. Restoration began in 1943 and is still being carried out today; the convent now also serves as a museum. The convent's foundation dates to 1726, making it the city's fourth, and is the work of renowned Antigua architect Diego de Porres. There are beautiful fountains and courtyards flanked by sturdy stone pillars with stately arches and flowering bougainvillea. It is certainly the most elegant of Antigua's convents and well worth a look for those with even a casual interest in colonial

Arco de Santa Catalina

Latin American architecture. The convent was the haunt of the Capuchin nuns from Madrid, a rather strict order limiting its numbers to 28 and requiring the nuns to sleep on wooden beds with straw pillows and sever all ties to the outside world.

The church consists of a single nave lacking side aisles. There are two choir areas, one adjacent to the altar on the ground floor and another on the second floor at the end of the nave.

After the 1773 earthquakes and the subsequent transfer of the Guatemalan capital to its new location, many of the convent's historical artifacts were likewise transferred to their new home in the San Miguel de Capuchinas convent in modern-day Guatemala City.

Iglesia y Convento de Santa Clara

The Iglesia y Convento de Santa Clara (2a Avenida Sur #27, 9am-5pm daily, $4) originally dates to 1702, with its current incarnation having been inaugurated in 1734 and destroyed in 1773. The convent ruins are also pleasant for a stroll, and in front of its main entrance is **Parque La Unión** with several wash basins, known as *pilas,* where women gather to do their laundry. The park's other outstanding feature is a large stone cross, a gift from the city of Santiago de Compostela, Spain. The church is beautifully floodlit at night.

Iglesia de San Francisco

Southwest on 1a Avenida Sur, the **Iglesia de San Francisco** (8am-6pm daily) is one of Antigua's oldest, dating to 1579. It once harbored a hospital, school, printing press, and monastery, among other things. Its main claim to fame nowadays is the tomb of Central America's first saint, **Hermano Pedro de San José Betancur,** a Franciscan monk who came to Antigua from the Canary Islands and founded the Hospital de Belén. He is credited with miraculous healings. The **Museo del Hermano Pedro** (8am-5pm, $0.50) is found on the south side of the church along with

the ornate La Merced church

the ruins of the adjacent monastery. It houses church relics and some of Hermano Pedro's well-preserved personal belongings.

Iglesia y Convento de Nuestra Señora de la Merced

Known more commonly as **La Merced** (5a Avenida Norte and 1a Calle Poniente, 9am-6:30pm, $0.50), this is one of Antigua's most beautiful churches, painted in a bright yellow and adorned with white lily motifs on its columns. Inside are the ruins of its old monastery with the Fuente de Peces, said to be the largest fountain in Latin America and interestingly in the shape of a water lily. The pools were once used for breeding fish. The upper level affords some wonderful city views, and the fountain just outside the church is also worth a look.

Iglesia y Convento de la Recolección

On Avenida de la Recolección, the large **Iglesia y Convento de la Recolección** built between 1701 and 1715 was heavily damaged in 1717 in the same year it was inaugurated. The earthquakes of 1773 finished the job, and it has lain in ruins ever since.

MUSEUMS
Museo de Arte Colonial

On the former site of San Carlos University, the **Museo de Arte Colonial** (5a Calle Oriente #5, tel. 7832-0429, 9am-4pm Tues.-Fri., 9am-noon and 2pm-4pm Sat.-Sun., $3.50) harbors sculptures of saints, murals, furniture, and colonial paintings by Mexican artists. A beautiful Moorish courtyard dominates the surviving architecture.

★ Centro Cultural Casa Santo Domingo

Antigua's finest museum is housed inside the Casa Santo Domingo hotel: **Centro Cultural Casa Santo Domingo** (3a Calle Oriente #28, tel. 7832-0140 or 7820-1220, www.casa-santodomingo.com.gt, 9am-6pm Mon.-Sat., 11:15am-6pm Sun., $5). The site was once the city's largest and wealthiest monastery, with

Semana Santa in Antigua

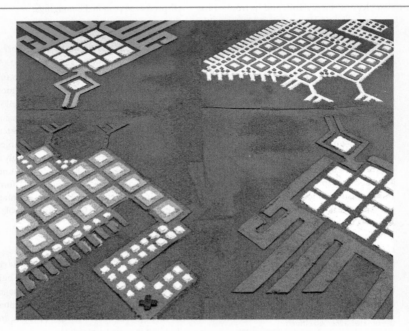

Semana Santa, or Holy Week, runs from Palm Sunday to Easter Sunday and is one of the best times to visit Antigua for the elaborate Catholic pageantry surrounding these holy days. Visitors come from around the world to see the colorful, solemn processions in which life-sized images of Christ and other Catholic icons are paraded through the city's cobblestone streets. Before the processions pass through, Antigueños design and produce exquisite, though ephemeral, *alfombras,* or carpets made of colored sawdust and flowers. The parade floats, or *andas,* pass over the carpets, forever erasing their elaborate patterns under the feet of faithful *cucuruchos,* purple-clad bearers who carry the floats. The floats can weigh up to 3.5 tons and require 80 men to carry them. The bearers are accompanied by Roman soldiers and other robed figures who carry swaying, copal-laden incense burners. It can be quite a moving experience to see the swaying floats with images of a cross-bearing Christ bearing down on the men amid thick smoke.

A highlight of the week's festivities is a Good Friday event occurring at 3am in which Roman soldiers on horseback gallop through the streets proclaiming Christ's death sentence. Though several local churches participate in the festivities, the largest procession is the one leaving from La Merced on Good Friday with the 17th-century image of Jesús Nazareno (Jesus of Nazareth). Another well-known procession is that of the Escuela de Cristo, which features some striking images on its parade floats.

For specifics on Holy Week events, head to the INGUAT office (corner of 2a Calle Oriente and 2a Avenida Norte, 8am-12:30pm and 2:30pm-5pm Mon.-Fri., 9am-12:30pm and 2:30pm-5pm Sat.-Sun.) on the central plaza, where you'll find free maps and event schedules. If you plan to take in the festivities, book far in advance, as word about Antigua's Holy Week events has been out for quite some time and accommodations fill up several months ahead with foreign visitors and vacationing Guatemalans.

a church completed in 1666, but it was damaged and eventually destroyed by the 18th-century earthquakes. Several museums are housed within the same complex, including the colonial museum harboring Catholic relics, among them an old Roman coin found during the excavations for the hotel's construction. Other highlights of this wonderful historic complex include a gorgeous monastery church, cleared of rubble and restored in the early 1990s. It is now frequently used for weddings. Below this area are two crypts. The first of these, the Cripta del Calvario, has a well-preserved Crucifixion mural. The other crypt harbors two graves with human bones.

There is also a small archaeological museum, but the highlight here is the Museo Vigua de Arte Precolombino y Vidrio Moderno, a fantastic, well-presented juxtaposition of colonial and pre-Columbian artifacts mixed with glass art. Rounding out the impressive list of attractions is the Casa de la Cera, an elaborate candle shop.

★ Casa Popenoe

Authentically restored to recreate the living conditions of a 17th-century official, Casa Popenoe (1a Avenida Sur #2, tel. 2338-7959, www.casapopenoe.ufm.edu, by appointment only with a minimum of six people, 8am-4pm Mon.-Fri., 8am-11am Sat., $10) was originally built in 1762 by wealthy merchant Venancia López Marchán upon the ruins of two homes from 1650. Like much of Antigua, it was left abandoned after the 1773 earthquakes until Dr. Wilson Popenoe and his wife, Dorothy, bought it in 1929. Dr. Popenoe, an agricultural scientist, worked with the United Fruit Company for much of his career and had a long history of adventures in plant collecting and botany in addition to his painstaking restoration of this fantastic cultural monument. He died in 1975, but two of his daughters continued to live in the house, one the noted archaeologist Marion Popenoe Hatch. The house was eventually donated to Guatemala's Francisco Marroquín University. You'll see paintings of Bishop Francisco Marroquín and fierce conqueror Pedro de Alvarado. Also on display are the wonderfully restored servants' quarters and kitchen. A narrow staircase leads up to the roof terrace, from where there are gorgeous views of Antigua and the volcanoes off in the distance.

Entertainment

NIGHTLIFE

Antigua has a lively nightlife scene, particularly on weekends when wealthy youths from Guatemala City flood the city streets in search of a good time.

Bars

Always popular with the American expat crowd is Café No Sé (1a Avenida Sur #11C, tel. 7832-0563, www.cafenose.com, 6pm-1am daily), where you can enjoy drinks in a charmingly gritty setting, often with live music. There's also good pub grub, though the main attraction is the tequila/mezcal bar, featuring their very own brand, Ilegal Mezcal. The secondhand bookstore next door is open until 6pm. A welcome new addition to the town's pub scene is The Snug (6a Calle Poniente #14, tel. 4215-9601), where you'll find cheap beers and a fun, cozy atmosphere.

Monoloco (5a Avenida Sur #6, tel. 7832-4228, ext. 102, www.restaurantemonoloco.com, 11am-1am daily) is also wildly popular and lively. It's set on two floors, and you can drink alfresco on the second-floor terrace. Reasonably priced burgers, nachos, and pizzas are served, and there are sports on the downstairs TV.

An old standby for grabbing a drink and watching the sunset with nice volcano views is the rooftop bar at Café Sky (corner of 6a Calle and 1a Avenida, tel. 7832-7300, 8am-1am daily). In addition to the rooftop terrace café bar, there's the downstairs Sky Lounge and Bamboo Bar, where you can enjoy drinks and a full menu of tasty food that includes sandwiches, lasagnas, and quesadillas.

Another popular watering hole, **The Ocelot Bar** (4a Avenida Norte #3, tel. 7832-1339, 12:30pm-1am daily), enjoys a prime location near the central plaza. There's often live jazz and blues in addition to a weekly Sunday evening pub quiz. Upstairs and under the same ownership is **Lava Terrace Bar,** with nice views of the surroundings from shady patio umbrellas and scrumptious gourmet burgers made from imported Angus beef. Happy hour is at 5pm daily.

A few blocks south of the park, **La Sala** (6a Calle Poniente #9, tel. 7832-9524) hosts a fun mix of Guatemalans and foreigners. The ambience is modern with a splash of Guatemalan color. There's also a varied menu that runs the gamut from Indian chicken dishes to bangers 'n mash. Next door is the new incarnation of Antigua's original Irish pub, **Reilly's En La Esquina** (6a Calle Poniente #7, tel. 7832-6251).

Dancing

Antigua's most popular and dependably fun disco is the two-story **La Casbah** (5a Avenida Norte #30, tel. 7832-2640, www.lacasbahantigua.com, 7pm-1am Thurs.-Sat., $4 cover), where you can dance the night away in a classy atmosphere popular with the wealthy Guatemala City crowd. The admission price includes one drink. **La Sin Ventura** (5a Avenida Sur #8, tel. 7832-0581) is a popular disco bar with mostly Latin music and dancing on weekend nights. There are a number of nightclubs in and around 6a Avenida Sur popular with the weekend crowds. Just follow the sound of music. Highly recommended is **Las Vibras** (Calle del Arco Casa #30, tel. 7832-3553, noon-1am daily) for its cool club vibe, dance floor, and very tasty food that make for a fun night out with friends. Down the street is **Sunset Terrace** (6a Avenida Norte #1C, tel. 5945-6640), which functions as a restaurant by day but gets increasingly more crowded (and raucous) as the night goes on. There are sometimes live dj sets.

Live Music

Restaurante Las Palmas (6a Avenida Norte #14, tel. 7832-9734, www.laspalmasantigua.com) has live Latin music on Friday and Saturday nights starting at 9:30pm. **Mesón Panza Verde** (5a Avenida Sur #19, tel.

The Ocelot Bar

7955-8282, www.panzaverde.com) features live jazz and Latin music nightly 8pm-10pm.

CINEMA

On the edge of town on the way to Santa Ana, La Casa del Río (Calle del Hermano Pedro #6, tel. 7832-5438) is a cultural center opened by two Guatemalan actors. There's a screening room where independent films and Guatemalan cinema are shown. It's worth checking out.

Shopping

Antigua is one of Guatemala's top places for shopping, with a wide assortment of excellent shops carrying quality items not found elsewhere in the country. You'll be hard-pressed to find the same variety of home decor, textiles, clothing, and jewelry anywhere else. Don't feel you have to confine your purchases to what you can fit in your checked airline baggage allotment, as there are a number of local companies that can help you ship your loot home.

HANDICRAFTS

Antigua's Mercado de Artesanías (4a Calle Poniente Final, 8am-7pm) is an attractive, safe place to shop for textiles, handicrafts, and souvenirs among several stalls. There is also an adjacent outdoor market selling fruits, vegetables, and wonderful fresh flowers. Textura (5a Avenida Norte #33, tel. 7832-5067, 10am-5:45pm Mon.-Wed., 10am-6:45pm Thurs.-Sat., 10am-5pm Sun.) sells stylish home furnishings in updated versions of Mayan textiles, including gorgeous hammocks and table dressings. Selling similarly exquisite indoor and outdoor home furnishings is El Telar (5a Avenida Sur #7, tel. 7832-3179, www.eltelar-antigua.com).

Nim Po't (5a Avenida Norte #29, tel. 7832-2681, 9am-9pm daily) has a large selection of traditional Mayan dress items, including colorful *huipiles* (blouses), *cortes* (skirts), and *fajas* (belts). There is also a wide variety of artwork, souvenir T-shirts, tourist trinkets, masks, and other wooden carvings in the spacious warehouselike setting. Just down the street, Nativo's (5a Avenida Norte #25B, tel. 7832-6556, 10am-7pm daily) also sells textiles and has some extremely rare, beautiful, and no-longer-produced textiles in the $600 range. Ask to see them. Quinta Maconda (5a Avenida Norte #11, tel. 7832-1480 or 5309-1423, www.quintamaconda.com, 9:30am-1pm and 2pm-7pm daily) sells its own brand of high-quality handcrafted leather travel gear and handwoven Guatemalan brocades in beautiful muted hues and earth tones. It also has a fine collection of Southeast Asian antiques and wooden furniture in its by-appointment-only showroom. One of my favorite shops for high-quality (though somewhat expensive) crafts and textiles is Colibrí (4a Calle Oriente #3B, tel. 7832-0280, textilescolibri@turbonett.com, 9am-6pm daily). I particularly like their bedspreads, though a queen size will set you back about $200.

For gifts to bestow upon loved ones back home, head to Atypical Treasures (3a Calle and 4a Avenida #7A, tel. 7832-0467, 9am-7pm Mon.-Sat., noon-6pm Sun.), a well-curated selection of local handicrafts interwoven with hard-to-find items from regions like Cobán. There's also a fine assortment of beautiful women's clothing (original designs) and handbags made from reclaimed Guatemalan *huipiles* that you can purchase for a song.

JEWELRY

Guatemala produces some of the world's finest jade, including rare black jade, found only in this part of the world. You can buy fabulous jade jewelry here tax-free. The best store for perusing wonderful jade creations in colorful hues, including emerald, yellow, and lilac, is **Jade Maya** (4a Calle Oriente #34, tel. 7931-2400, www.jademaya.com, 9am-7pm daily), where you'll find a vast array of items varying from 18-karat gold/jade earrings to a unique $3,800 jade chess board. All of the jade found here is mined from a quarry in eastern Guatemala. The store doubles as a jade museum, and you can also visit the factory behind the shop. Guided tours are available in German, Spanish, English, French, and Italian. For fashionable and exotic jewelry, handbags, and sunglasses, visit **Joyería del Ángel** (4a Calle Oriente #5A, tel. 7832-3189, www.delangel.com, 9am-6pm daily). For silver jewelry, check out **Pablo's Silver Shop** (5a Calle Poniente #12C, tel. 7832-8960).

BOOKS

Hamlin y White (4a Calle Oriente #12A, tel. 7832-7075, 9am-6:30pm daily) has a good selection of books and international magazines. Under the same ownership is **Tiempo Libre** (5a Avenida Norte #25, tel. 7832-1816, 9am-7pm daily), with a wider assortment of books in English and Spanish, including Moon Handbooks. On the west side of the plaza in the Portal del Comercio, **La Casa del Conde** (5a Avenida Norte #4, tel. 7832-3322, 9am-7pm Mon.-Sat., 10am-7pm Sun.) sells an assortment of travel guides in addition to material specifically relating to Guatemala, Central America, and the Mayan world, mostly in English. **Dyslexia** (1a Avenida Sur #11, tel. 5162-4515, 1pm-6pm daily) has a good selection of secondhand books curated by its scribe owners who publish *La Cuadra* magazine.

ART, ANTIQUES, AND FURNITURE

Panza Verde (5a Avenida Sur #19, tel. 7955-8282, www.panzaverde.com) is a gallery housed inside its namesake restaurant/hotel; a new exhibit usually opens every second Wednesday of the month. **La Antigua Galería de Arte** (4a Calle Oriente #15, tel. 7832-2124, www.laantiguagaleria.com,

Colibri's colorful coaster designs

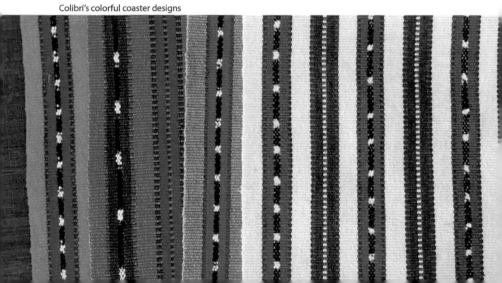

9am-7pm Mon.-Sat.) exhibits the work of numerous local and international artists in a large building surrounding a pleasant courtyard. Casa de Artes (4a Avenida Sur #11, tel. 7832-0792 and 7832-1390, www.casadeartes.com.gt) is like a museum chock-full of textiles, masks, jewelry, and other wonderful finds where the items are available for purchase.

For antique furniture and architectural accents, a good bet is Ritual (7a Calle Poniente #30, tel. 7832-4767, www.ritualstyle.com). Casa Chicob (5a Avenida Norte #31, tel. 7832-0781, www.casachicob.com, 9am-6pm Mon.-Sat.) features a wonderful assortment of Guatemalan-inspired home decor and luxurious personal care products. Uxibal (Callejón del Sol Casa #9, tel. 7832-7417, www.uxibal.com) sells fashionable leather shoes, boots, handbags, and accessories incorporating Guatemalan textiles.

COFFEE AND TOBACCO

For coffee, head to Tostaduría Antigua (6a Calle Poniente #26, tel. 7832-5159, tostaduriaantigua.blogspot.com). You can buy Cuban and Honduran cigars, as well as enjoy them in a comfortable lounge, at Antigua Tabaco Compañía (3a Calle Poniente #12, tel. 7832-9420, 10am-10pm daily).

WELLNESS

One of Antigua's most interesting stores is La Tienda de Doña Gavi (3a Avenida Norte #2, tel. 7832-6514, noon-7pm daily), where you can pick up a number of natural remedies, including Jacameb, a powerful concoction created from the jacaranda flower that does the trick on amoebas and assorted other parasitic problems. (Friendly Doña Gavi also serves the tastiest mango ice cream I've ever had.) Organic groceries, natural foods, and eco-friendly products can be found at Orgánica (5a Calle Poniente #6, tel. 7832-6533, 8am-6pm daily).

Caoba Farms (5a Avenida Sur final, tel. 7758-9510 or 7832-9201, www.caobafarms.com, 8am-5pm Mon.-Fri., 8am-noon Sat., 9am-1pm Sun.) sells organic produce cultivated on several plots of land in the Antigua area. They also brew their own kombucha. Tours to the farms are available (see website for details) at a cost of $10 per person. Volunteer opportunities are available.

Caoba Farms

Recreation

HEALTH CLUBS

Antigua's Gym (6a Calle Poniente #31, tel. 7832-7554, 6am-9:30pm Mon.-Fri., 7am-3pm Sat., 8am-3pm Sun.) offers spinning, Tae Bo, cardiovascular equipment, free weights, and some weight-lifting machines. **La Fábrica** (1a Avenida Norte #7A, tel. 7832-9840) also has cardiovascular machines and weights in addition to aerobics and rock climbing. My gym of choice is **Equinox** (Carretera a Ciudad Vieja, tel. 7832-2957, 5am-9pm Mon.-Fri., 6am-3pm Sat., 8am-1pm Sun.). It's a somewhat large facility with plenty of equipment, classes, and parking out front.

SPAS AND YOGA

Casa Madeleine (Calle del Espíritu Santo #69, tel. 7832-9348, www.casamadeleine.com/spa) offers complete spa packages along with its swanky boutique hotel accommodations. Services include massage, reflexology, aromatherapy, mud therapy, pedicures, manicures, and deep facial treatments. **Healing Hands** (3a Avenida Norte #20A, tel. 7832-1648, www.healinghandsguatemala.com) is a well-run day spa offering the usual assortment of spa services in a pleasant environment. There are overnight accommodations and a yoga studio.

There are quality yoga classes by trained U.S. instructors available in Antigua. **YogAntigua** (tel. 5251-4809, www.yogantigua.com) offers classes every morning inside **Galería Panza Verde** (5a Avenida Sur #19) and afternoons at Calle del Hermano Pedro #16. Vinyasa and Hatha yoga classes start at $10 for drop-in or $32 for a five-class pass.

MOUNTAIN BIKING

Antigua's mountain terrain and the variety of trails traversing it make mountain biking a popular recreational activity. **Old Town Outfitters** (5a Avenida Sur #12, tel. 7832-4171, www.adventureguatemala.com, 9am-6pm daily) is a highly recommended outfitter offering rides for all skill levels. Half-day options include easy rides in the Almolonga Valley or in and around coffee plantations to edge-of-your-seat single-track rides careening down volcanic slopes or along narrow mountain ridges with fantastic views. Its equipment is top-notch and well cared for. **Guatemala Venture** (1a Avenida Sur #15, end of 6a Calle Oriente, tel. 7832-6264, www.guatemalaventure.com, 9am-6pm daily) is another recommended outfitter for tackling the rugged terrain around Antigua by mountain bike. It also rents out mountain bikes for $8 a day. Both companies also offer a lot of other recreational options in addition to mountain biking, as you'll see by the frequency with which they are mentioned here.

O.X. Outdoor Excursions (7a Calle Poniente #17, tel. 7832-0468, www.guatemalavolcano.com) has cornered the market on "cool" with the addition of mountain biking to its arsenal of adventurous offerings. Trip options range from cycling around Antigua's neighboring villages to adrenaline-inducing single-track careens down volcanic slopes. They also rent mountain bikes for $22 a day.

BIRD-WATCHING
Finca El Pilar

Just a 45-minute walk from Antigua's central park (or a 10-minute *tuk-tuk* ride), **Finca El Pilar** (tel. 7832-4937, fincaelpilar@live.com, 6am-6pm daily, $5) is a private reserve protecting a large area that includes dry forest, pine oak, and cloud forest. Among the bird species you can expect to find are numerous types of rare and endemic hummingbirds, emerald toucanet, golden-browed warbler, highland guans, and blue-throated motmot. There is a system of trails and observation platforms throughout the reserve and altitude ranges from 5,250 to 7,870 feet. To get here, walk south from the central plaza toward 7a Calle until you reach San Francisco

Church. Behind the church, you'll find the path leading to neighboring Santa Ana. Look for El Calvario church, where you'll turn left and continue all the way to the end of an uphill path, passing San Cristobal El Bajo church along the way. Cayaya Birding (tel. 5308-5160, www.cayaya-birding.com) does guided trips to the reserve. If you get tired of hiking, you can take a leisurely soak in the swimming pool ($1.50).

★ Finca El Zapote

Outside of town, along the road to Escuintla, is this Eden-like botanical garden situated on the slopes of active Fuego Volcano. Finca El Zapote (Aldea Guadalupe, Escuintla; tel. 5000-1899, www.fincazapote.com, $20 adults, $9 children) has been owned by the local Pettersen family since the late 1950s. Mr. Pettersen geared the farm toward quinine production, but Mrs. Pettersen, a renowned artist and author of *The Maya of Guatemala: Life and Dress*, used her considerable talents and British education to create Guatemala's most amazing botanical gardens. Birds naturally find this exotic locale, between the Pacific Coast lowlands and volcanic highlands, a very welcoming place, and there are numerous species in evidence including magpie jays,

several species of egret, herons, and woodpeckers. The views of Fuego Volcano alone are worth the price of admission, but the beautifully manicured lawns and 25 acres of luxuriant tropical foliage could easily be the envy of better-known European botanical gardens. There's a spring-fed swimming pool for refreshment and four lagoons for fishing.

Two different houses are available for rent if you choose to stay here (highly recommended). The Estate House ($575-800) sleeps up to 14 guests, while the more modest Lake House ($300-400) sleeps six. You'll need a high clearance vehicle to get here even in dry season, as it's a rough road that at times is impassible during the rainy season. Transfers from Antigua are sometimes available by request.

HIKING

There is no shortage of rugged hiking trails for enjoying the spectacular mountain scenery and peaceful mountain villages found near Antigua. The same recommended mountain biking outfitters can point you to the best hiking trails. A guide is highly recommended, as robberies of solo hikers along remote mountain footpaths is sometimes an issue in rural Guatemala. The bulk of the hiking done

the Lake House at Finca El Zapote

around Antigua involves one of the volcanoes towering ominously over its streets.

★ Volcano Climbs

At 3,750 meters (12,325 feet) **Agua Volcano** is one of Antigua's most visible volcanoes with its near-perfect crater that looms just south of Antigua. Unfortunately, its slopes have been plagued by safety issues for years. All of the local outfitters, tired from numerous instances of robberies, have ceased hikes up the volcano.

Just shy of 4,000 meters (13,044 feet), **Acatenango Volcano** is a safer and somewhat more interesting climb. It's an intense six-hour ascent through agricultural fields and cloud forests on sandy gravel. Most of the outfitters camp at a spot 500 meters from the summit. From there it's a grueling final push to the summit on the steepest part of the volcano (and the sandiest). It's worth the effort, however, as your reward is a spectacular view of active **Fuego Volcano** right next to it. You won't find better views of Fuego and the experience is quite unique, as no other volcano in Central America is quite like this. **Old Town Outfitters** (5a Avenida Sur #12, tel. 7832-4171, www.adventureguatemala. com, 9am-6pm daily) offers a one-day or overnight trip to the volcano starting in the village of La Soledad, from where it's a 5-6-hour hike through cornfields and pine forests to the crater. A newer option is that of taking a 4x4 through private lands en route to a spot just two hours' hike from the summit. **Guatemala Venture** (tel. 7832-6264, www. guatemalaventure.com) also does this trip.

By far the most popular volcano trip is to active **Pacaya Volcano,** near Lake Amatitlán and closer to Guatemala City. There's no shortage of outfitters offering this trip, which generally leaves in the afternoon and costs $7-30 per person. Recommended companies include **Old Town Outfitters** (5a Avenida Sur #12, tel. 7832-4171, www.adventureguatemala.com, 9am-6pm daily), which leaves earlier than most other companies to avoid the crowds. **Adrenalina Tours** (3a Calle Poniente #2D, tel. 7882-4147 or 5308-1489, www.adrenalinatours.com) leaves daily at 6am and 2pm. The trip costs $10 and includes round-trip transportation and local Spanish-speaking guide. The more expensive VIP trip costs $75 and leaves whenever you want it to. The VIP tour includes bilingual and local guides, transportation, park admission, and breakfast.

Personally recommended for all of the

hikers running along the crater of Acatenango Volcano

Fire on the Mountain

Looming over Lake Amatitlán and the Guatemala City valley is the 2,552-meter-high active Pacaya Volcano (www.volcandepacaya.com) spewing lava and ash for the amazement of tourists and locals alike. Its current active phase began in 1965 and has barely ceased since. Activity varies from quiet gas, lava, and steam emissions to full-scale explosive eruptions hurtling rocks into the sky. It sometimes spews large ash clouds that prompt the closure of Guatemala City's La Aurora International Airport, as was the case when a 1998 eruption blanketed the airport runway in fine volcanic sand and again in May 2010.

Guatemala is one of few places in the world where you can get up close and personal with an active volcano in relative ease. While the climb is not for the faint of heart, adventurous types will find it to be a worthwhile endeavor. The volcano makes a convenient day trip from Guatemala City (45 minutes) or Antigua (1 hour). Logistically, it makes more sense from Guatemala City, but the tour operators offering the trip are almost entirely based in the old colonial city. It's possible to make the trip on your own, though going in a group with a local guide is highly recommended.

The volcano's national park status dates to 2001. A visitor's center and ticket booth can be found at the trailhead in the village of San Francisco de Sales. Admission to the park is $5. You can also hire a guide here. There is safe parking for vehicles in San Francisco de Sales, and the well-maintained trail has good signage, rest stops with trash receptacles, and outhouses. Park rangers patrol the trails and incidents of robbery, which once plagued this otherwise wonderful place, have become virtually unheard of since 2001.

From the town of San Francisco de Sales, the 3.7-kilometer trail up Pacaya Volcano (2-3 hours) climbs gradually through cornfields and secondary forest before arriving at a vast volcanic wasteland of old lava flows. After crossing a barren ridge, the trail then winds up the slopes of the volcanic crater itself. Hiking up the loose ash will give you the sensation of taking two steps forward and one step back. It's a good workout but worth the effort. At the summit, you're treated to a fine view of the main vent spewing lava, rocks, and ash. It may sometimes feel too close for comfort, as large chunks of lava rock often land nearby. Take a moment to glimpse Guatemala City, the Pacific Coast, and some of the neighboring volcanoes from here.

At the summit, avoid breathing in the clouds of sulfuric gases. Be especially careful where you step, as there are some hot zones and sometimes some slow-moving lava flows. The skilike descent down the same sandy ash can be tricky, and you should exercise due caution to avoid a nasty face-plant into the jagged lava rocks alongside the trail.

If hiking during the day, bring plenty of sunscreen along with a hat, preferably with a chin strap that will prevent it from blowing away at the windy summit. Water and some snacks are always a good idea. Try not to carry excessive amounts of cash, but just what you'll need for the park admission, guide tip, and a drink and/or snack when you arrive back at the base of the trail. Rain gear (depending on the season) and some good, sturdy boots are also important. You'll especially appreciate the latter because you'll need ankle support and it's easy to get rocks and sand in your shoes, which can be extremely uncomfortable, during the final ascent up the sandy crater.

To get here on your own steam, follow the CA-9 highway past Amatitlán to a signed turnoff at Km. 37.5. Head east eight kilometers to the village of San Vicente Pacaya, where you'll find the park entry station and information center. The road continues from here another 10 kilometers to San Francisco de Sales (turn left at the fork in the road just past San Vicente Pacaya). For an excellent map detailing the route of ascent, see the interactive map online at *Mapas de Guatemala* (www.mapasdeguatemala.com/mapas).

above trips is O.X. Outdoor Excursions (7a Calle Poniente #17, tel. 7832-0468, www.guatemalavolcano.com), offering well-guided trips to the Antigua area volcanoes. The Spires of Fire trip is a five-day adventure climbing Guatemala's three active volcanoes (Fuego, Pacaya, and Santiaguito); it costs $599. They also do a very challenging "Double Whammy" involving the ascent of Acatenango Volcano with a side trip to Fuego Volcano on the same day before arriving (exhausted) to Vista Camp for bed and the summit of Acatenango the next morning.

CANOPY TOURS

The zipline madness that seems to have gripped almost every tourist town in Central America has not bypassed Antigua. If you want to monkey around, zipping from tree to tree, your best bet is **Antigua Canopy Tours** (tel. 7728-0811, www.antiguacanopytours. com, $50-75). For the ultimate adventure, try its Canyon Express tour across a canyon in two stages (520 and 430 meters long) while dangling 500 feet above the ground. The zipline tour is located on the property of Finca Filadelfia, near Jocotenango.

HORSEBACK RIDING

In the nearby village of San Juan del Obispo, toward Agua Volcano, **Ravenscroft Riding Stables** (2a Avenida Sur #3, San Juan del Obispo, tel. 7830-6669) offers three-, four-, or five-hour rides in the hills and valleys near Antigua for $20 per person per hour.

CITY TOURS

Practically an Antigua institution, **Antigua Tours** (3a Calle Oriente #22, tel. 7832-5821 and 7832-2046, www.antiguatours.net) are guided by Elizabeth Bell (author of *Antigua Guatemala: The City and Its Heritage*) Tuesday, Wednesday, Friday, and Saturday at 9:30am. Tours on Monday and Thursday at 2pm are led by other experienced guides. All tours meet at the fountain in Antigua's central park and cost $25, including entrance fees to historical sites. There is also a guided tour of nearby villages, including San Antonio Aguas Calientes, San Pedro Las Huertas, and San Juan del Obispo, going out at 2pm Tuesday and Friday and lasting three hours. It costs $35 per person with a two-person minimum. Advance booking required.

Green Belly Adventure Co. (Callejón San Sebastián #2B, tel. 7832-1669, www.green-bellyadventure.com, $50-65 per person) offers tours of Antigua's historical sites and local coffee farms aboard off-road versions of Segways. It actually makes a great way to get around Antigua's narrow cobblestone streets.

GOLF

Antigua is home to Guatemala's newest—and nicest—golf course, the 18-hole Pete and Perry Dye-designed **Fuego Maya golf course** at **La Reunión Antigua Golf Resort** (RN-14 Km. 93, Alotenango, tel. 7873-1400, www.

Fuego Maya golf course at La Reunión Antigua Golf Resort

to the 19th hole.) The golf course is 11 miles from Antigua and 40 miles from Guatemala City. Facilities include a driving range, putting green, chipping green, practice bunker, and pro shop.

WINE TASTING

Ever exciting and brimming with new leisure opportunities, Antigua Guatemala now boasts Guatemala's first winery. **Chateau DeFay** (tel. 2363-3858 or 5883-3911, www.fincade-fay.com), on the slopes of Agua Volcano in neighboring Santa María de Jesús, is a 3,000-case winery and vineyard. Its owners, Jacques and Angie Defay, purchased a former coffee farm and converted part of the land into vineyards using plants brought in from Washington state. The farm also grows asparagus. Jacques, a former economist with the International Development Bank (IDB), retired to Guatemala from Falls Church, Virginia, in 2002 after numerous visits to the country.

The winery is open for tastings Saturday and Sunday 10am to 4pm. Chateau DeFay wines come in several varieties, including Angie's Blend, chardonnay, a moscato, a cabernet sauvignon/merlot blend, and Bruno's Favorite. The latter is named for resident winemaker Bruno Coppola.

The first year of wine production was 2008, but the 2009 vintage is substantially better. A bottle of wine costs between Q130 and Q190, or about $16-25.

Chateau DeFay vineyards

lareunion.com.gt). The 72-par, 7,560-yard course is one of the country's most challenging and is the only golf course in the world with a view of four volcanoes (Agua, Fuego, Acatenango, and Pacaya). Its designers gleaned inspiration from the Mayan Solar Calendar, which consists of 18 20-day months; each of the course's 18 holes is named after the corresponding month. (The last month, Wayeb, is a five-day month and gives its name

Accommodations

UNDER $50

Antigua has a number of excellent hostels offering comfortable accommodations at budget prices. Most of them can help you arrange onward travel or book airport shuttle services if they don't offer it themselves. A favorite budget traveler hangout is friendly ★ **Terrace Hostel** (3a Calle Poniente #24B, tel. 7832-3463, www.terracehostel.com, $9

in shared-bath dorm to $30 d in room with shared bath). Included are the usual amenities found in most hostels such as luggage storage, laundry service, wireless Internet, TV, DVD collection and library, but Terrace Hostel goes the extra mile with a fun rooftop bar and restaurant. There's a nightly barbecue featuring hot dogs, burgers, nachos, and chili you can wash down with local microbrews. There are weekly pub crawls and occasional theme parties. **Jungle Party Hostel** (6a Avenida Norte #20, between 3a and 2a Calle Poniente, tel. 7832-8975, www.junglepartyhostal.com, $10-11 pp) is a lively backpacker hangout with clean dorm rooms and shared baths. There are fun communal areas that double as bar and lounge.

Conveniently located near some of the town's favorite watering holes, **El Hostal** (1a Avenida Sur #8, tel. 7832-0442, www.elhostal.hostel.com, $12-18) has cozy private rooms with shared bath ($18 d) or clean, shared-bath dormitories ($12 pp) in a remodeled colonial house that includes a pleasant little courtyard. Guests won't find electric water heaters here (yippee!), but rather the hot-water showers many visitors are used to. You can book and pay online in advance; wireless Internet is available throughout the house.

A rooftop chill-out area with wonderful views of Agua Volcano and a friendly, feel-good vibe make ★ **Holistico Hostal** (7a Avenida Sur #10, tel. 7832-4078, www.hostalholistico.com, $11 pp in dorm to 40 d with private bath) a popular choice. The nightly rate includes breakfast, served in its small café. There is free wireless Internet, a movie lounge, and laundry service for $2.50 per load. Tours to local attractions can be arranged. They also have decent hot-water showers.

Just one block from the central plaza, **Hotel Casa Rústica** (6a Avenida Norte #8, tel. 7832-0694, www.casarusticagt.com, $35-56 d) has comfortable rooms with shared bathroom ($39-45 d) or private bathroom ($49-56 d), with or without cable TV and garden view. There are apartments for rent starting at $250 per week. Rates include breakfast, filtered drinking water, and use of the kitchen. It also offers laundry service, bag storage, and wireless Internet. There are nice gardens and hammocks for lounging. The excellent-value ★ **Casa Cristina** (Callejón Camposeco #3A, between 6a and 7a Avenida, tel. 7832-0623, www.casa-cristina.com, $25-45 d) has beautifully decorated, colorful rooms with wrought-iron accents, Guatemalan bedspreads, tile

floors, and private hot-water bathroom. Pricier deluxe rooms have gorgeous volcano views and minifridges, in addition to cable TV. TVs are absent in the least expensive standard rooms. Room rates include unlimited use of wireless Internet, purified drinking water, coffee, and tea. The excellent-value **Hotel Posada San Pedro** (3a Avenida Sur #15, tel. 7832-3594, www.posadasanpedro.net, $41 d) is also stylish and comfortable, featuring 10 spotless rooms with firm beds, tile floors, wooden furnishings, attractive tile bathrooms, and cable TV. Guests also enjoy use of a living room and full kitchen. The staff here is friendly, and the place is well-run with a laid-back but efficient atmosphere. There's a second location at 7a Avenida Norte #29 (tel. 7832-0718, $46 d) with slightly higher rates for newer rooms.

$50-100

One of the city's best values is ★ **Chez Daniel** (Calle de San Luquitas #20, tel. 4264-1122, chezdanielantigua.blogspot.com, $59 d). It's seven blocks from the central square in a quiet neighborhood, in a large house fronting a green lawn. The comfortable, high-ceilinged rooms have flat-screen TVs and large bathrooms with shower tubs. They are wonderfully decorated with Guatemalan knickknacks and amazing photography depicting the country's vivid Maya culture. Amenities include a dining room, fully equipped communal kitchen, and rooftop terrace with volcano views. Featuring many of the fine decorative touches and amenities of its pricier boutique counterparts ★ **El Mesón de María** (3a Calle Poniente #8, tel. 7832-6068, www.hotelmesondemaria.com, $85-140 d on weekdays; $15-20 higher on weekends) is a good value. Its 20 brand-new, well-appointed rooms are attractively decorated with Guatemalan fabrics and beautifully carved wooden headboards. You'll feel the antique charm as soon as you enter the doorway of your room framed with antique wooden beams. Rooms on the second floor have skylights and some of the spacious tiled bathrooms have whirlpool tubs.

La Antigua Guatemala Accommodations

CALLE DEL BURRO

CALLE DEL ESPÍRITU SANTO

CALLE DE SAN LUCAS N

CHEZ DANIEL

CALLE DEL RANCHÓN

CALLE DEL DESENGAÑO

IGLESIA Y CONVENTO DE LA RECOLECCIÓN

CALLE DE RECOLETOS

2A AVENIDA DE CHAJÓN

MERCADO DE ARTESANÍAS

TERRACE HOSTEL

2A CALLE P

CALLE DE LA SANGRE DE CRISTO

7A CALLE P

7A AVE. S

HOLÍSTICO HOSTAL

HOTEL CASA RÚSTICA

6A AVENIDA S

CALLE SUCIA

6A CALLE P

CAMINO REAL ANTIGUA

4A CALLE P

POSADA LA MERCED

CALLE CAMPOSECO

CALLE DE LOS NAZARENOS

CASA CRISTINA

JUNGLE PARTY HOSTEL

1A CALLE P

6A AVENIDA N

ARCO DE SANTA CATALINA

IGLESIA Y CONVENTO DE NUESTRA SEÑORA DE LA MERCED

To Filadelfia Coffee Resort

CANCHA DE LOS HERREROS

EL MESÓN DE MARÍA

5A AVENIDA N

QUINTA MACONDA

PARQUE CENTRAL

4A AVENIDA S

HOTEL POSADA DE DON RODRIGO

4A AVENIDA N

PORTA HOTEL ANTIGUA

MESÓN PANZA VERDE

9A CALLE O

8A CALLE O

D'LEYENDA HOTEL

IGLESIA Y HOSPITAL SAN PEDRO

CATEDRAL DE SANTIAGO

IGLESIA Y CONVENTO DE LAS CAPUCHINAS

MIL FLORES

2A AVENIDA N

EL CONVENTO

1A CALLE O

HOTEL POSADA SAN PEDRO

2A AVENIDA S

CASA POPENOE

6A CALLE O

4A CALLE O

2A AVENIDA S

IGLESIA Y CONVENTO DE SANTA CLARA

EL HOSTAL

CALLE DE LA NOBLEZA

HOTEL QUINTA DE LAS FLORES

7A CALLE O

IGLESIA DE SAN FRANCISCO

CALLEJÓN DE LA CONCEPCIÓN

CALLE DE SANTO DOMINGO

CENTRO CULTURAL CASA SANTO DOMINGO

CALLE DEL HERMANO PEDRO

To Posada El Ensueño

HOTEL CASA SANTO DOMINGO

Río Pensativo

0
0

200 yds
200 m

POSADA DE LOS LEONES

HOTEL CIRILO

There are gorgeous views of the town and volcanoes from the delightful third-floor terrace. Rates include breakfast at the nearby La Fonda de la Calle Real.

For a phenomenal location at an incredible price, it's hard to beat ★ D'Leyenda Hotel (4a Avenida Norte #1, tel. 7832-6194, www.dleyendahotel.com, $90-110 d). The hotel is less than a block from the central square. Its somewhat smallish but comfortable rooms are named after different Antigua ghost legends and include flat-screen cable TV, safe deposit box, and wireless Internet. Three of its six rooms have bathtubs and fireplaces. A fountain graces the ground floor courtyard opposite a spiral staircase leading to a second-floor terrace with lounge chairs, tables, a hot tub, and volcano views. It bears mentioning that there's a popular watering hole next door, as that may or may not suit your style. Did I mention the staff is extremely friendly?

OVER $100
Resorts

Antigua's newest resort hotel is the ★ Camino Real Antigua (7a Calle Poniente #33B, www.caminorealantigua.com.gt, $145-210 d). The chain hotel has cozy rooms with high, wood-beamed ceilings and some of the most delicious beds I've ever slept on, as well as all the amenities you would expect.

A *Condé Nast Traveler* Gold List property, Porta Hotel Antigua (8a Calle Poniente #1, tel. 7931-0600, www.portahotels.com, from $125 d) has 77 sumptuous rooms with chimneys, colorful walls with faux finishes, Guatemalan decor, and charming stained hardwood floors in its standard and deluxe rooms and suites. It features a restaurant serving excellent Guatemalan and international dishes overlooking the swimming pool set amid tropical gardens, as well as a fully stocked, quaint wooden bar. Candles provide atmosphere at night and a colonial fountain graces the entrance to the hotel. The service is excellent, as is the courteous and friendly staff. Another property that has put Antigua on the map of the world's finest accommodations is the exquisite ★ Hotel Casa Santo Domingo (3a Calle Oriente #28, tel. 7820-1220, www.casasantodomingo.com.gt, $150-550 d), built in the ruins of an old Dominican monastery. Its 125 rooms have all the comforts you could wish for and effortlessly merge colonial charm with modern comfort. Some rooms have a chimney, and there are some newer rooms with chic glass and wooden showers. Other amenities include a charming swimming pool and a location just steps from the city's best museum and wonderful colonial ruins. The restaurant here is also highly recommended.

Boutique Hotels

Antigua has an astounding assortment of boutique properties offering comfort and privacy in an atmosphere of elegance and style. Spending a night in one of Antigua's boutique properties is the real deal and can feel like waking up in a museum chock-full of interesting knickknacks and artwork. Posada de Don Rodrigo (5a Avenida Norte #17, tel. 7832-9858, www.posadadedonrodrigo.com, $150 d) is one of Antigua's classic hotels, well situated near the Arco de Santa Catalina. Housed in a very old residence, the inviting rooms have been updated with all the comforts of a modern hotel. The staff wears traditional costumes and marimba music can often be heard in the main courtyard. President Clinton chose ★ Posada del Ángel (4a Avenida Sur #24A, tel. 7832-0260 Antigua or 305/677-2382 U.S., www.posadadelangel.com, from $195 d) for his 1999 visit to Antigua for a summit meeting with Central American leaders. If you'd like to follow in his footsteps, stay in the exquisite Rose Suite, the largest of the lodge's five, with a private balcony offering gorgeous volcano views and fine antiques. Each of the suites is different, but all are truly charming and include wood-burning fireplace, cable TV, and fresh flowers. Rates include a delicious breakfast served in the dining room looking out to the hotel's small lap pool.

Mil Flores Luxury Design Hotel (3a

El Convento boutique hotel

is sometimes the haunt of international celebrities. El Convento (2a Avenida Norte #11, tel. 7720-7272, www.elconventoantigua.com, from $169 d) is fabulously built on grounds across the street from Convento de las Capuchinas. All 26 of its well-appointed suites are unique and feature a magnificent melding of colonial and modern touches that include skylights, bathrooms with marble and glass accents, exposed stone walls, and charming courtyard patios. There is a wonderful second-floor terrace for enjoying cocktails (or Sunday breakfast buffet), and the vaulted-ceiling dining room at Elù Restaurant on the main floor serves gourmet Guatemalan fusion cuisine.

An excellent value in this category, ★ Hotel Cirilo (Calle de los Duelos #11, tel. 7832-6650, hotelcirilo.com, from $119 d) combines modern touches with the charm and history of La Antigua. Built on the grounds of an old hermitage, the property features spacious gardens, old ruins, and a wooden-decked swimming pool. Glass doors provide wonderful views of the grounds from the

Calle Oriente #16A, tel. 7832-9715 or 7832-9716, www.hotelmilflores.com, from $175 d including breakfast) offers style with distinction, excellent service, and attention to detail. Each of the five luxurious suites is inspired after a different flower and features a fireplace, minibar, a private patio, and large bathroom.

One of Antigua's most elegant properties, ★ Posada de los Leones (Las Gravileas #1, tel. 7832-7371, www.posadadelosleones.com, $280-380 d) is set amid coffee trees and tropical gardens in a gated community just outside of town. Its six spacious, absolutely gorgeous rooms feature high ceilings, hardwood floors, and a delightful array of classy European and Guatemalan decorative touches. On the house's second floor is Antigua's loveliest terrace overlooking tropical gardens, the surrounding coffee plantation, and the volcanoes off in the distance. You can enjoy drinks on the terrace in addition to a lap pool, a comfortable living room, and library. There is wireless Internet throughout the house, which

the swimming pool at Hotel Cirilo

comfortable living room and breakfast areas. Some of the comfortable rooms are literally built around the old ruins, and you can have the old architecture all to yourself. Other room features include *retablo* headboards, a fireplace, and flat-screen TV. It's quietly outside of the town center.

OUTSIDE OF TOWN

On a working 40-acre avocado farm, **Earthlodge** (tel. 5664-0713 or 4980-2564, www.earthlodgeguatemala.com, dorms $8 pp to $45 d in cabin) is a sure bet for wonderful volcano views and the chance to get away from it all at a reasonable distance from town in the surrounding hillsides. Accommodations include a shared-bath, eight-bed dormitory, A-frame cabins, and tree houses. The private cabins and tree houses are wonderfully secluded in a grove of Spanish oaks and have fabulous views of the valley and surrounding mountains. There are shared or private bathroom options and queen or double beds.

Delicious vegetarian dinners are served family-style for $9, though carnivores need not despair as meat options are also available, including a fun weekend barbecue. Breakfast items include eggs, bacon, sausage, pancakes, and fresh fruit. Heaping sandwiches and salads are served for lunch. You can relax in a hammock and take in the valley views, hike nearby trails, or sweat out any remaining pre-vacation stress in the stone-and-mortar sauna. There are also books, movies, music, and games on hand should you need further entertainment. Spanish classes and massages are also available. The easiest way to get here is via the lodge-designated transfers from Antigua with a local driver. Rates start at $7 per person, one-way.

Also in the hills above Antigua in the area of El Hato is one of Guatemala's most unique hotels. **Hobbitenango** (tel. 5909-9106, camping $2.50, dorm $8 pp, $52 for 5-person cottage) takes its inspiration from J. R. R. Tolkien's fictional Hobbiton (of Lord of the Rings fame). It is still very much a work in progress, but its creators have focused their efforts on providing a place to get off the grid amid a spectacularly scenic location overlooking the Antigua valley. The property prides itself in environmentally sustainable practices, such as the use of recycled materials for construction, rainwater collection, organic farming, and wind/solar power generation. The accommodations mimic the homes of Tolkien's Shire-dwelling hobbits, and there's a restaurant/bar with wonderful views. A light menu is served weekdays, with a full menu on weekends. There are also shuttle transfers from downtown Antigua Friday through Sunday.

Outside the city center on the way to Santa Ana is **Hotel Quinta de las Flores** (Calle del Hermano Pedro #6, tel. 7832-3721/25, www.quintadelasflores.com, $75-140 d), another excellent value. The lodge was built on the site of what were once public baths, and you can still hear the soothing sounds of tinkling fountains throughout the property. The charming rooms, built around a peaceful and spacious garden, feature tile floors, chimneys, cable TV, Guatemalan bedspreads, and nice accents and furnishings along with a small porch with sitting area. Larger two-bedroom casitas comfortably sleep five and have living room, dining room, and fully equipped kitchen. There's a large outdoor swimming pool just next to the hotel's restaurant, which serves Guatemalan dishes, including delicious *chuchitos* and *tostadas,* or salads, steak, and chicken. It's a good choice for vacationing families. Also in Santa Ana, ★ **Posada El Ensueño** (Calle del Agua, Callejón La Ermita Final, Santa Ana, tel. 7832-7958, www.posadaensueno.com, $100-125 d) is a splendid bed-and-breakfast in a quiet setting. Run by American expatriate Carmen Herrerias, the lodge has three tastefully decorated rooms with garden showers, one of which is a suite. It's a great place to relax away from the action in Antigua. Breakfast and home-cooked meals are served poolside, and Carmen loves to cook for her guests. There's also a small heated lap pool and bikes to get around. It's about a 25-minute walk to Antigua's central park.

Just minutes from Antigua in neighboring San Felipe de Jesús, ★ **Filadelfia Coffee Resort and Spa** (150 meters north of the San Felipe de Jesús church, tel. 7728-0800, www.filadelfiaresort.com, $125-250 d including breakfast) is a working coffee farm where you can stay in a splendid neocolonial building harboring luxurious accommodations. The 20 spacious rooms have tile floors, king- or queen-size beds, classy Guatemalan furnishings, cable TV with DVD player, large two-sink bathrooms, glass showers with antique tiles, and pleasant patios with furniture. There are four standard rooms, 14 deluxe doubles, and two master suites with island kitchen and a living room with leather sofa and large desk. Coffee machinery and wooden carvings adorn the public areas, while the main building harbors a cozy lobby adorned with Persian rugs. An elegant restaurant in the main lodge serves international dishes with flair. Activities include daily coffee tours lasting two hours each at 9am, 11am, and 2pm ($18), mule riding ($15-40), paintball ($20-40), and a unimog ride to a lookout point ($20). There are free unimog transfers from Antigua's town center if you want to take a tour or just enjoy a meal here.

Opened in 2008, ★ **La Reunión Antigua Golf Resort** (Km. 91.5 Carretera CA-14, tel. 7873-1400, www.lareunion.com.gt, $220 d) lies 17 kilometers from Antigua in neighboring Alotenango on the road to the Pacific Coast. The hotel setting and its Pete Dye-designed 18-hole golf course is truly spectacular, flanked by four volcanoes and lush green fields. The larger suites are worth the splurge (an extra $50 over the deluxe rooms), for their private infinity-edge plunge pools and a hot tub with stunning volcano views (Agua and active Pacaya). The luxuriously well-furnished rooms have L'Occitane bath products, air-conditioning, and satellite TV. For dining, there's the resort's Mirador restaurant serving international fare, a snack bar, and Bar Wayeb. Plans call for the existing 26-room boutique hotel to be joined by a 125-room hotel managed by an international hotel chain. For now, La Reunión remains wonderfully peaceful. The only sounds you'll hear are the chirping of birds, the occasional roar of a distant lawnmower, and, once in a while, a landing helicopter announcing the arrival of Guatemala City's business elite coming in for a round of golf. It's all par for the course.

La Reunión Antigua Golf Resort

Food

Antigua's status as one of Guatemala's main tourist destinations is evident in the variety and number of excellent restaurants for every taste and budget. The mix here is rather eclectic, and restaurants can often be classified into more than one category. While the presence of a McDonald's in town hardly constitutes anything worth writing home about, Antigua's golden arches are the focus of some local lore completely in line with the magic seemingly everywhere in Guatemala. According to local urban legend, the Ronald McDonald sitting on the bench outside Antigua's McDonald's has at least on one occasion uncrossed its legs and come to life, scaring two employees sweeping the patio out of their wits.

CAFÉS AND LIGHT MEALS

★ **The Refuge** (7a Avenida Norte #18A, www.refugecoffeeroasters.com, 7:30am-7pm Mon.-Sat., $3) is an independent coffee shop serving phenomenal coffee and espresso beverages at very reasonable prices in a quaint, intimate atmosphere. Also recommended for its high-quality coffee is **Tretto Caffe** (1a Avenida Sur #4, tel. 4828-0692, 7:30am-8pm daily). For coffee on the go, **Café Barista** (on *parque central's* northwest corner) serves a variety of favorites, including caramel macchiato, mochas (hot or iced), and tasty pastries. It's part of a chain popular throughout Guatemala. One of Antigua's best-known cafés, **Doña Luisa Xicotencatl** (4a Calle Oriente #12, tel. 7832-2578, 7am-9:30pm daily) serves delicious breakfasts, snacks, pastries, and light meals in a delightful garden courtyard. There are fresh-baked breads and cakes available all day from the bakery at the front of the building. Next door, **La Fuente** (4a Calle Oriente #14, tel. 7832-4520, 7am-7pm daily) is a good place for breakfast and vegetarian fare as well as for a cup of coffee accompanied by an ever-so-sinfully delicious chocolate brownie topped with coffee ice cream and chocolate syrup.

On the west side of the central park, ★ **Café Condesa** (Portal del Comercio #4, tel. 7832-0038, 7am-8pm Sun.-Thurs., until 9pm Fri.-Sat.) is a great place to get some pep in your step with an early breakfast and coffee or to refuel later in the day. There are excellent cakes, pastries, sandwiches, and salads served in a pleasing garden atmosphere, or you can enjoy the all-day breakfasts. A Sunday brunch is served 10am-2pm and includes scrambled eggs, home-fried potatoes, silver-dollar pancakes, quiche, homemade bread, and muffins, just to name a few items. If you're on the go, grab a cup of the excellent coffee at the **Condesa Express** next door.

For fresh bagels, bagel sandwiches, and great coffee, stop at **The Bagel Barn** (5a Calle Poniente #2, tel. 7832-1224, www.the-bagelbarn.com, 6am-9pm daily). There is wireless Internet if you're traveling with a laptop, and movies are shown in the afternoons and evenings. Another Antigua standby is the **Rainbow Café and Bookshop** (7a Avenida Sur #8, tel. 7832-1919, www.rain-bowcafeantigua.com, all meals daily), serving delicious menu options including eggs Florentine, Israeli falafel, and the chocolate bomb for dessert. Try the outstanding Greek chicken fillet stuffed with spinach, bacon, raisins, feta cheese, and covered with a creamy oregano and lime sauce ($9). Live music, poetry readings, and other cultural events are held on-site. Under the same ownership as Café No Sé, ★ **Y Tu Piña También** (corner of 6a Calle Oriente and 1a Avenida Sur, www.ytupinatambien.com, $3-8) has evolved from its origins as a juice bar into a great all-day breakfast spot. There are awesome sandwiches, breakfast pizzas, salads, and of course, coffee. There's also no shortage of hangover-curing cocktails. Check out their Sunday brunch. Finally, a trip to Antigua wouldn't be complete without a stop for some *dulces típicos* (typical Guatemalan sweets) from **Doña**

La Antigua Guatemala Food and Nightlife

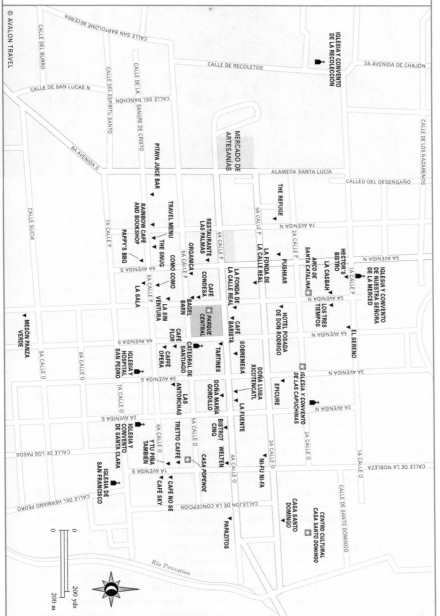

CALLE SAN BARTOLOMÉ BECERRA

CALLE DEL BURRO

CALLE DE RECOLETOS

2A AVENIDA DE CHAJÓN

IGLESIA Y CONVENTO DE LA RECOLECCIÓN

CALLE DE SAN LUCAS N

CALLE DEL ESPÍRITU SANTO

CALLE DEL RANCHO

CALLE DE LA SANGRE DE CRISTO

CALLE DE LOS NAZARENOS

8A AVENIDA S

MERCADO DE ARTESANÍAS

ALAMEDA SANTA LUCÍA

CALLED DEL DESENGAÑO

CALLE SUCIA

PITAYA JUICE BAR

THE REFUGE

7A CALLE P

3A CALLE P

2A CALLE P

7A AVENIDA N

6A AVENIDA N

TRAVEL MENU

RAINBOW CAFÉ AND BOOKSHOP

THE SNUG

RESTAURANTE LAS PALMAS

PUSHKAR

HÉCTOR'S BISTRO

LA CASBAH

IGLESIA Y CONVENTO DE NUESTRA SEÑORA DE LA MERCED

PAPPY'S BBQ

4A CALLE P

5A CALLE P

ORGÁNICA

ARCO DE SANTA CATALINA

7A AVENIDA S

6A AVENIDA S

COMO COMO

CAFÉ CONDESA

LA FONDA DE LA CALLE REAL

LOS TRES TIEMPOS

5A AVENIDA N

6A AVENIDA N

LA SALA

LA SIN VENTURA

BAGEL BARN

LA FONDA DE LA CALLE REAL

CAFÉ BARISTA

HOTEL POSADA DE DON RODRIGO

4A AVENIDA N

EL SERENO

MESÓN PANZA VERDE

9A CALLE O

8A CALLE O

CAFÉ FLOR

PARQUE CENTRAL

4A AVENIDA S

SOBREMESA

3A AVENIDA N

IGLESIA HOSPITAL SAN PEDRO

CAFÉ ÓPERA

CATEDRAL DE SANTIAGO

TARTINES

DOÑA LUISA XICOTENCATL

EPICURE

IGLESIA Y CONVENTO DE LAS CAPUCHINAS

7A CALLE O

3A AVENIDA S

LAS ANTORCHAS

DOÑA MARÍA GORDILLO

LA FUENTE

2A AVENIDA N

2A AVENIDA S

5A CALLE O

BISTROT CINQ

WELTEN

3A AVENIDA O

2A CALLE O

CALLE DE LA NOBLEZA

IGLESIA Y CONVENTO DE SANTA CLARA

6A CALLE O

TRETTO CAFFÈ

CASA POPENOE

NI-FU NI-FA

4A CALLE O

1A AVENIDA O

CALLE DE LOS PASOS

IGLESIA DE SAN FRANCISCO

Y TU PIÑA TAMBIÉN

CAFÉ NO SÉ

1A AVENIDA S

CASA SANTO DOMINGO

CENTRO CULTURAL CASA SANTO DOMINGO

CALLE DE SANTO DOMINGO

CALLE DEL HERMANO PEDRO

CAFÉ SKY

PAPAZITOS

CALLEJÓN DE LA CONCEPCIÓN

0   200 yds

0   200 m

Río Pensativo

Pappy's BBQ

María Gordillo (4a Calle Oriente #11, tel. 7832-0403). Under new ownership, **Travel Menu** (6a Calle Poniente #14, tel. 5682-9648, $5-10) is a budget traveler favorite for its tasty, varied menu that runs the gamut from steak to Asian cuisine at affordable prices.

Pitaya Juice Bar (6a Calle Poniente #26, tel. 7832-1172, www.pitayajuicebar.com, 8:30am-6pm Mon.-Sat., 9am-4pm Sun., $2-5) serves a variety of natural blended juices, smoothies, soups, salads, and wraps. All of the ingredients are amazingly fresh, and the atmosphere is cheerful and bright.

STEAKHOUSES

Ni-Fu Ni-Fa (3a Calle Oriente #21, tel. 7832-6579, www.nifunifadeantigua.com, noon-10pm Sun. and Mon., noon-10:30pm Tues.-Thurs., noon-11pm Fri. and Sat., $5-22) is a genuine Argentinean steakhouse serving tasty grilled meats on a pleasant raised wooden deck surrounded by lush gardens. **Restaurant Las Antorchas** (3a Avenida Sur #1, tel. 7832-0806, www.las-antorchas.com, 11am-3pm and 6pm-10pm Mon.-Fri., 11am-4pm and 6pm-10pm Sat., 11am-5pm Sun., $8-31) offers a more elegant setting and a menu that includes grilled onions, cheese fondue, tortellini, salmon in orange sauce, and well-presented grilled steak and chicken dishes.

AMERICAN

Sometimes during long visits to Guatemala I get a little homesick for the taste of Texas. Thank goodness for **Pappy's BBQ** (6a Calle Poniente #21, tel. 7832-2768 or 5979-6771, www.bbqantigua.com, 11am-10pm Tues.-Sat., 11am-8pm Sun., $3-9), serving authentically tasty Texas barbecue. On the menu are several Texas favorites including mouthwatering coffee-rubbed beef brisket, pork ribs, pulled pork, smoked chicken, and smoked pork sausage. The latter, while on the menu, is in fact rarely available (which is my only complaint about this otherwise awesome dining option). Side dishes include potato salad, Texas baked beans, and spicy corn on the cob. It's a casual, friendly kind of place. There are delicious homemade sauces to bring out the meats' delicious flavors.

CONTINENTAL

Antigua is full of hidden gems. One of these is ★ **Hector's Bistro** (1a Calle Poniente #9A, tel. 7832-9867, lunch and dinner, $7-17), tucked away on the street fronting Iglesia La Merced. It's a simple kind of place with half a dozen tables and a bar. The menu rotates but includes amazing open-faced sandwiches, homemade pasta, seared duck, and beef tenderloin. You can watch your meal being prepared in the open kitchen. Olives make a wonderful starter to pair with a glass of wine. ★ **Como Como** (6a Calle Poniente #6, tel. 7832-0478, lunch and dinner Tues.-Sun., $5-20) specializes in Franco-Belgian cuisine and enjoys a loyal following thanks to consistently great food and a pleasant atmosphere that includes a lovely garden patio. **Sobremesa** (4a Calle Oriente #4A, tel. 7832-3231, www.alexferrar.com, $8-13) is a restaurant doubling as an art gallery. The art is fabulously eclectic, but the food is not to be outdone. Menu highlights include phenomenal croque-monsieur, delicious Unicorn Steak (tenderloin medallion in a wine and Dijon reduction), and yummy Japanese Plum Chicken. For dessert, savor exotic ice cream flavors the likes of strawberry merlot and jasmine blackberry. Antigua's finest delicatessen is **Epicure** (3a Avenida Norte #11 B, tel. 7832-5545, 10am-10pm daily, $5-12), serving phenomenal sandwiches and deli items. The owners prefer that patrons dine on-site rather than carry out, and the pleasant outdoor area centered around a lovely garden courtyard and the remains of an old aqueduct makes that request easy to accommodate. A second location (6a Avenida Norte #35 A, tel. 7832-1414) is only open until 7pm Monday-Saturday (until 6:30pm Sun.).

Extremely popular with Antigua's expat community for its wonderful views over town, laid-back vibe, and fresh farm-to-table vegetarian fare is **Cerro San Cristóbal** (tel. 7832-2681, 9am-9pm daily). The menu includes dishes such as stuffed mushrooms, quiche, and frittatas. You can tour the on-site organic farm and a lovely orchid nursery. There are frequent (and free) shuttle transfers from Nim Po't, located at 5a Avenida Norte #29.

Enjoying a new lease on life from its new location, **Caffé Opera Bistrot** (4a Avenida Sur #1, tel. 7832-9133, www.caffeoperabistrot.com, noon-3:30pm and 6:30pm-10pm Mon.-Tues. and Thurs., noon-11pm Fri.-Sat., noon-10pm Sun., $6-12) serves up tasty Italian food, including homemade pasta. For gourmet pizza, try **Papazitos** (4a Calle Oriente #39, tel. 7832-5209, 11am-10pm daily). It also serves nachos, panini, calzones, pastas, vegetarian dishes, wine, and beer. It offers free delivery with a minimum $7 purchase; 10- to 18-inch pizzas go for $9-16.

GUATEMALAN AND LATIN AMERICAN

One of Antigua's legendary restaurants is **La Fonda de la Calle Real** (3a Calle Poniente #7, tel. 7832-0507, www.lafondadelacallereal.com, noon-10pm daily; 5a Avenida Norte #5, tel. 7832-2696, noon-10pm daily; 5a Avenida

chips and salsa at Los Tres Tiempos

Norte #12, tel. 7832-0507, 8am-10pm daily, $5-12), with three branches, the nicest of which is the one on 3a Calle Poniente. There is a varied menu of Guatemalan favorites, including *chiles rellenos* as well as tasty grilled meats. If you can't decide, do as President Clinton did and order the filling sampler menu. For gourmet Guatemalan cuisine served in a stylish environment with modern Guatemalan decor, head to **Los Tres Tiempos** (5a Avenida Norte #21, tel. 7832-5161, www.lostrestiempos.com, 8am-10pm daily, $5-12). There are delicious enchiladas, *chuchitos,* and tacos to be enjoyed in a spacious second-floor patio with funky lounge chairs or inside in comfortable *huipil*-inspired seats. There's a cozy and equally stylish little downstairs bar if you're just stopping by for a cocktail.

ASIAN

Café Flor (4a Avenida Sur #1, tel. 7832-5274, www.cafeflorantigua.com, 11am-11pm daily, $6-12) does a reasonably good job with Thai food, though it won't taste familiar to diehard fans of Asian cuisine. Offerings include Thai curries and rice dishes. For Indian food, check out **Pushkar** (6a Avenida Norte #18, tel. 7882-4098, lunch and dinner daily, $4-11). You'll find several of your Indian favorites on the menu, including meat or vegetable samosas, seafood curries, chicken tikka masala, and tandoori chicken. There's also pleasant outdoor patio seating. For decent Chinese food, head to **Restaurante La Estrella** (7a Avenida Norte #42, tel. 7832-4303). They also deliver.

FINE DINING

One of the city's most atmospheric restaurants, **El Tenedor del Cerro** (tel. 7832-3520, 7am-10pm Mon.-Sat., 7am-5pm Sun., $4-15) features fabulous views of the Antigua valley and its volcanic backdrop, along with a well-rounded menu that includes hearty breakfasts, salads, pasta, pizzas with an interesting array of international flavors, steaks, and decadent desserts. Many of the fresh ingredients come straight from the on-site garden. The views of Agua, Fuego, and Acatenango Volcanoes are fully appreciated with outdoor seating on a pleasant patio. There are a

the courtyard at Mesón Panza Verde

separate patio lounge, gift shop, aviary, and sculpture gardens to enjoy, along with rotating art exhibits. To get here, follow the winding road to the top of the hill. The entrance is just before Antigua's main entrance, on the left, on the road from Guatemala City. There are also free transfers from Hotel Casa Santo Domingo.

With a long tradition of excellence, Welten (4a Calle Oriente #21, tel. 7832-0630, www.weltenrestaurant.com, noon-10pm Mon.-Thurs. and Fri.-Sun. until 10:30pm, $13-22) is one of Antigua's well-established dining options serving an impressive menu of gourmet Guatemalan, French, and Italian specialties in an elegant atmosphere. Menu highlights include creamy peppered steak (filet au poivre), seafood fettuccine, and fish fillet in a traditional salsa. There are delicious homemade ice creams for dessert. ★ Mesón Panza Verde (5a Avenida Sur #19, tel. 7955-8282, www.panzaverde.com, lunch Tues.-Sun., dinner 7pm-10pm nightly, $10-30) is easily one of Guatemala's finest restaurants, with outstanding food and sophisticated European ambience. The mostly French cuisine is heavy on meat and fish dishes. The wine list is impressive, as are the desserts. Tapas are served 4pm-7pm Thursday-Saturday on the terrace. You can enjoy lunch and dinner in the main dining room surrounded by fine art under a vaulted ceiling or alfresco in La Cueva, a covered patio beneath baroque arches beside a gurgling fountain. *Chacun à son goût.*

The town's most authentic hotel restaurant can be found at ★ Hotel Posada de Don Rodrigo (5a Avenida Norte #17, tel. 7832-0291, all meals daily, $7-20), which is popular with Guatemalans who come here for its stellar service, wonderful ambience overlooking the hotel gardens, and consistently delicious Guatemalan and international cuisine. The tortillas are made fresh on the premises, and you can watch the dough being patted and placed on the *comal,* where it is cooked over a fire. There is sometimes live marimba music to complete the authentic Guatemalan feel.

A longtime favorite is ★ El Sereno (4a Avenida Norte #16, tel. 7832-0501, www.elserenoantigua.com, lunch and dinner daily, $9-25). The restaurant dates to 1980, but the wonderfully old colonial building in which it's housed dates to the 16th century and once housed the Spanish priests who built La Merced church. You can dine on gourmet international dishes in the elegant main dining room, in a romantic cavelike candlelit room, or alfresco either in a delightful covered garden patio or on the rooftop terrace.

Last but certainly not least of the fine dining options is ★ Bistrot Cinq (4a Calle Oriente #7, tel. 7832-5510, www.bistrotcinq.com, noon-10pm daily, until 11 Fri./Sat., $9-25). The emphasis is on French cuisine; dishes include chicken scaloppine and trout Armandine, but with take-out or delivery items such as scrumptious half-pound burgers and steak *frites* also on the menu. The bar is top-notch and includes absinthe.

Information and Services

TOURIST INFORMATION

The INGUAT office (5a Calle Oriente #11, tel. 7832-0787 or 2421-2951, 8am-5pm Mon.-Fri., 9am-5pm Sat.-Sun.), also known as Casa del Turista, has friendly, helpful staff who can help steer you in the right direction as well as provide free maps, bus schedules, and other useful information. A useful website with lots of information on hotels, restaurants, shops, and services is www.aroundantigua.com. Another useful publication is the monthly *Revue* magazine, available free at many hotels, restaurants, and shops. Another publication, *Qué pasa en Antigua,* has very complete information on all that's going on.

The Giant Kite Festival

If you're visiting the Antigua or Guatemala City area around November 1, you should certainly plan a trip to either of the highland Mayan towns of Santiago Sacatepéquez or Sumpango, home to the annual Giant Kite Festival. In addition to the lively atmosphere of a typical Mayan fiesta, you'll be treated to an awe-inspiring display of larger-than-life kites, typically 20-50 feet wide. The kites are painstakingly crafted from tissue paper and bamboo reeds incorporating colorful and elaborate designs. Preparations typically begin six weeks in advance, in mid-September, with teams working extended hours as the deadline for completion draws closer. Judges are on hand at the festival to name the best entries in a variety of categories.

Kites under 20 feet in diameter are flown over the town cemetery later in the day and are believed to be a vehicle for speaking with the souls of departed loved ones. The flying kites are representative of the floating spirits of the dead. Larger kites are only for show and typically carry a message or theme, sometimes overtly political in nature. The weather is typically windy during this time of year, with the surrounding hillsides still tinged with verdant hues thanks to the recently ended rainy season. The colorful cemetery structures and the typical native dress of the Mayan people cap off a Technicolor dream of a day.

The festival in Sumpango, the larger of the two towns, takes place in a broad field adjacent to the cemetery. Santiago Sacatepéquez has a somewhat more cramped setting, its cemetery being perched on the edge of a plateau and extending down a gently sloping hillside. Personally, I prefer Sumpango's version of the event. For a mere three dollars, you can purchase access to bleacher seating, which gets you some nice vantage points for photography. In the afternoon, around 3pm, the official festivities begin with a speech by the local mayor and other such pageantry. The highlight of the afternoon is watching the giant six-meter kites take flight as teams of kite fliers test their skills and the sturdiness of their creations. Only kites six meters across in diameter or smaller are able to take flight, though you'll find plenty of larger kites on display. The difficulty of getting these monstrosities to become airborne is exacerbated by the large crowds, which leave little room for participants to do the necessary running to get the kites going. As a result, you'll

COMMUNICATIONS

Antigua's main post office is near the bus terminal on the corner of 4a Calle Poniente and Calzada de Santa Lucía and is open 9am-5pm. There are also various international couriers with offices here, including DHL (Corner 6a Calle Poniente and 6a Avenida Sur #16, tel. 2339-8400, ext. 7515). A number of companies can also help you ship home any purchases you're unable to fit in your check-in baggage allotment. These include Envíos Etc. (3a Avenida Norte #26, tel. 7832-1212), which is also the local representative for FedEx.

MONEY

Banco Industrial (5a Avenida Sur #4), just south of the plaza, has a Visa/Plus ATM. There is also an ATM on the north side of the plaza next to Café Barista. Another ATM may be found on the plaza's west side next to Café Condesa (Portal del Comercio #4). Avoid any and all BAC ATM machines, as there have been incidents of card cloning originating at their Antigua locations.

LAUNDRY

Detalles (6a Avenida Norte #3B, tel. 7832-5973, 7:30am-6:30pm Mon.-Sat., 8am-4pm Sun.) does dry cleaning and has coin-operated laundry machines. Lavandería Dry Clean (6a Calle Poniente #49, 7am-7pm Mon.-Sat., 9am-6pm Sun.) charges about $4 a load. Quick Laundry (6a Calle Poniente #14, tel. 7832-2937, 8am-5pm Mon.-Sat.) charges about $0.85 per pound.

often see the kites plunging quickly toward the crowd. It's all part of the fun, but it's also one more reason I prefer the bleacher seats off to the side. Many Antigua travel agencies offer special trips and shuttle transport to both towns on these days, or you can go by public bus. Santiago Sacatepéquez lies a few kilometers off the Pan-American Highway. You can take a direct bus from Antigua or get off from any Guatemala City-bound bus at the junction and continue from there. For Sumpango, your best bet is to get to Chimaltenango, also on the Pan-American Highway, and connect from there. Be prepared for huge crowds. If you drive your own vehicle, you'll likely need to park outside of town and walk uphill from the highway to the festival grounds.

EMERGENCY AND MEDICAL SERVICES

For the **Bomberos Municipales** (Municipal Fire Department), dial 7831-0049. **Casa de Salud Santa Lucía** (Calzada de Santa Lucía Sur #7, tel. 7832-3122) is a private medical hospital with 24-hour emergency services. **Hospital Nacional Pedro de Betancourt** is a public hospital two kilometers from town with emergency service. For serious issues, your best bet is to go to Guatemala City.

TRAVEL AGENCIES

Travel agencies are ubiquitous in Antigua. Among the recommended companies for shuttle buses is **Atitrans** (6a Avenida Sur #7, tel. 7832-3371, www.atitrans.net). For plane tickets and general travel needs, recommended travel agents include **National Travel** (6a Avenida Sur #1A, tel. 2247-4747), **Viajes Tivoli** (4a Calle Oriente #10, Edificio El Jaulón, tel. 7832-4274), and **Rainbow Travel Center** (7a Avenida Sur #8, tel. 7931-7878, www.rainbowtravelcenter.com).

Sin Fronteras (3a Avenida Sur #1A, tel. 7720-4400, www.sinfront.com) is another good all-around agency with package deals to Tikal in addition to local tours. It rents cars through Tabarini Rent A Car. **Bon Voyage Guatemala** (6a Avenida Norte #3A, tel. 7823-9209, www.bonvoyageguatemala.com) is a good source of travel information and acts as a booking agent for various transportation providers. The company also runs daily shuttles at 8am for El Salvador beaches. Also recommended for countrywide tours from Antigua is **Guinness Travel** (6a Avenida Norte #16, tel. 4623-6297, www.guinness-travel.com).

Choosing a Language School

Antigua has close to 100 language schools, and the task of choosing the right one can seem downright daunting. It really boils down to the quality of individual instructors, though some schools are definitely better than others. Look around and ask plenty of questions. If you decide midway through a weeklong course that you're just not jiving with the instructor, don't hesitate to pull out and ask for a new one. That being said, the following websites can help you out in your search: www.guatemala365.com and www.123teachme.com. Both have surveys and rankings of individual schools in Guatemala.

Among the recommended Antigua schools are **Academia de Español Antigueña** (1a Calle Poniente #10, tel. 7832-7241, www.spanishacademyantiguena.com), a small, well-run school with space for 10 students at a time. I've personally had the pleasure of working with **Spanish School La Unión** (1a. Avenida Sur #21, tel. 7832-7757, www.launion.edu.gt). They offer quality one-on-one instruction and are involved in a variety of social projects. **Escuela de Español San José El Viejo** (5a Avenida Sur #34, tel. 7832-3028, www.sanjoseelviejo.com) has its own very attractive campus where you can stay in comfortable accommodations with facilities that include a tennis court and swimming pool amid lovely gardens and coffee trees. A longtime student favorite is **Christian Spanish Academy** (6a Avenida Norte #15, tel. 7832-3922, www.learncsa.com), a very well-run school set in a pleasant colonial courtyard. Antigua's oldest language school is **Proyecto Lingüístico Francisco Marroquín** (7a Calle Poniente #31, tel. 7832-2886, www.plfm-antigua.org), run by a nonprofit foundation working toward the study and preservation of Mayan languages. It comes highly recommended. **Academia de Español Probigua** (6a Avenida Norte #41B, tel. 7832-2998, www.probigua.conexion.com) is run by a nonprofit group working to establish and maintain libraries in rural villages. Another good choice with comfortable accommodations across the street from the school is **Centro Lingüístico Internacional** (1a Calle Oriente #11, tel. 7832-0391, www.spanishcontact.com).

The recommended schools range in price $140-225 per week, including 20-35 hours of instruction and a stay with local family. While the schools provide everything you will need to learn the language, it might be a challenge to have a total language immersion experience because of the overwhelming presence of foreigners in Antigua. If this is an issue for you, consider taking Spanish classes in Cobán or Petén.

VOLUNTEER WORK

Although it's based in the city of Quetzaltenango, **EntreMundos** (www.entremundos.org) has a very useful database of volunteer projects throughout Guatemala. If you're interested in working with impoverished children, check out **The God's Child project** (U.S. tel. 612-351-8020, www.godschild.org).

COOKING SCHOOL

If you acquire a taste for traditional Guatemalan cuisine and want to re-create the country's myriad flavors at home, check out **El Frijol Feliz** (4a Avenida Sur #1, tel. 7832-5274, www.frijolfeliz.com, $30-45 per class). The school is open every day, and there are classes available in the morning or afternoon. The class includes instruction on the preparation of one main dish, two side dishes, and a dessert. More focused classes include instruction on the preparation of typical Guatemalan sauces such as mole and salsa verde. Dishes include *pepián, chiles rellenos,* and *chuchitos* (the author's favorite).

Transportation

BUS

The main **bus terminal** is found next to the market, three blocks west of the central plaza. It is separated from the heart of town by a broad, tree-lined street. There are connections to the highlands available by taking one of many frequent buses up to Chimaltenango (every 15 minutes, half-hour travel time) along the Pan-American Highway and a requisite stop for buses trundling along to the highlands from Guatemala City. You can also catch one of the slightly less frequent buses to San Lucas Sacatepéquez, which is closer to Guatemala City. There may be more seats available on the buses plying the same highway en route toward Chimaltenango. Buses for Guatemala City leave every 15 minutes or so 4am-7:30pm, taking about an hour and costing about $2. There is also a direct Rebuli bus to Panajachel at 7am leaving from the corner of Calzada Santa Lucía and 5a Calle Poniente (two hours, $5).

Otherwise, buses leave every 15 minutes for San Miguel Dueñas ("Dueñas," 30 minutes, $0.50) stopping along the way in Ciudad Vieja. There are also buses every 30 minutes for San Antonio Aguas Calientes and Santa María de Jesús.

SHUTTLE BUS

Many travelers opt for the comfort, convenience, safety, and hassle-free experience aboard one of the numerous shuttle buses. Destinations include frequent runs to the Guatemala City airport, at least one bus daily to Monterrico and Cobán, several daily to Panajachel and Quetzaltenango, and less frequently to Río Dulce. Recommended shuttle companies include **Atitrans** (6a Avenida Sur #7, tel. 7832-3371, www.atitrans.net) and **Adrenalina Tours** (3a Calle Poniente #2D, tel. 7882-4147, www.adrenalinatours.com).

the Antigua bus terminal

TAXI

Taxis can be found on the east side of the park next to the cathedral or by the bus terminal. The former is probably a safer place to board one. A ride to Guatemala City should cost around $30. You'll also see *tuk-tuks* (motorized rickshaws) throughout the city, costing considerably less and recommended for short distances.

CAR RENTAL

Hertz (7a Calle Poniente #33B, inside Camino Real Antigua hotel, tel. 3274-4420, www.rentautos.com.gt) has an office in Antigua, as does Budget (4a Avenida Sur #4, tel. 2203-2303, www.budget.com.gt). Tabarini (6a Avenida Sur #22, tel. 7832-8107) also rents cars.

BICYCLE RENTAL

O.X. Outdoor Excursions (7a Calle Poniente #17, tel. 7832-0468, www.guatemala-lavolcano.com) rents mountain bikes for $22 per day. You will need a passport and a valid credit card. Also for mountain bikes, check out Old Town Outfitters (5a Avenida Sur #12, tel. 7832-4171, www.adventureguatemala. com, 9am-6pm daily).

Near Antigua Guatemala

Antigua is surrounded by a number of picturesque towns and villages built in the midst of the Panchoy Valley and on the slopes of neighboring volcanoes. You'll find plenty of recreational opportunities in these parts—enjoy the region's natural backdrop, surrounded by coffee farms and even a winery.

JOCOTENANGO

Jocotenango lies just 3.5 kilometers northwest of Antigua. A pretty, pink stucco church adorns the main square. In colonial times, the town served as the official entry point into neighboring Antigua.

★ Centro Cultural La Azotea

The town's main attraction is Centro Cultural La Azotea (La Azotea Cultural Center, Calle del Cementerio, Final, tel. 7831-1486, www.centroazotea.com, 8:30am-4pm Mon.-Fri., 8:30am-2pm Sat., $4 adults, $0.85 children), which functions as a three-in-one coffee, costume, and music museum. The music museum, Casa K'ojom (www. kojom.org) features a wonderful assortment of traditional Mayan musical instruments, including *marimbas,* drums, a diatomic harp, and flutes in addition to masks and paintings collected by its dedicated administrator, Samuel Franco. There is also an audiovisual room where you can watch a video on traditional music as it would be played in Mayan villages. Traditional costumes and crafts of the Antigua Valley are exhibited in a separate room dedicated to Sacatepéquez department.

The adjoining Museo del Café covers the history and evolution of coffee cultivation and is available as a self-guided or guided tour. You can see coffee beans in varying stages of production from recently harvested to fully roasted. The well-illustrated displays include information on wet and dry mills, some old roasters, and machinery. You can then tour an actual plantation on-site. There is also a shop where you can buy CDs, DVDs, handicrafts, and of course, coffee.

Also found here is the Establo La Ronda (tel. 7831-1120), where you can ride around the grounds on horseback for an hour in the mornings ($3). Call ahead.

You can get to Jocotenango by taking any Chimaltenango-bound bus leaving from Antigua's bus terminal. Buses leave every 20 minutes; you can also take a *tuk-tuk* or taxi.

MAP SYMBOLS

≡≡≡	Expressway	○	City/Town	✈	Airport	⛳	Golf Course
≡≡≡	Primary Road	◉	State Capital	✦	Airfield	🅿	Parking Area
≡≡≡	Secondary Road	✸	National Capital	▲	Mountain	⛩	Archaeological Site
- - - -	Unpaved Road	★	Point of Interest	✚	Unique Natural Feature	⛪	Church
——	Feature Trail	•	Accommodation		Waterfall	⛽	Gas Station
- - - - -	Other Trail	▼	Restaurant/Bar	▲	Park		Glacier
··········	Ferry	■	Other Location	❶	Trailhead		Mangrove
≡≡≡	Pedestrian Walkway	△	Campground	⛷	Skiing Area		Reef
⊠⊠⊠	Stairs						Swamp

CONVERSION TABLES

°C = (°F – 32) / 1.8
°F = (°C x 1.8) + 32
1 inch = 2.54 centimeters (cm)
1 foot = 0.304 meters (m)
1 yard = 0.914 meters
1 mile = 1.6093 kilometers (km)
1 km = 0.6214 miles
1 fathom = 1.8288 m
1 chain = 20.1168 m
1 furlong = 201.168 m
1 acre = 0.4047 hectares
1 sq km = 100 hectares
1 sq mile = 2.59 square km
1 ounce = 28.35 grams
1 pound = 0.4536 kilograms
1 short ton = 0.90718 metric ton
1 short ton = 2,000 pounds
1 long ton = 1.016 metric tons
1 long ton = 2,240 pounds
1 metric ton = 1,000 kilograms
1 quart = 0.94635 liters
1 US gallon = 3.7854 liters
1 Imperial gallon = 4.5459 liters
1 nautical mile = 1.852 km

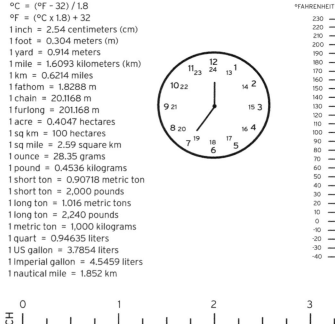

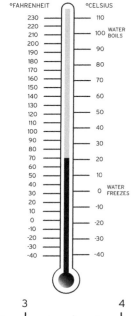

MOON SPOTLIGHT
GUATEMALA CITY & ANTIGUA

Avalon Travel
a member of the Perseus Books Group
1700 Fourth Street
Berkeley, CA 94710, USA
www.moon.com

Editor and Series Manager: Kathryn Ettinger
Copy Editor: Ashley Benning
Graphics Coordinator: Elizabeth Jang
Production Coordinator: Elizabeth Jang
Cover Design: Faceout Studios, Charles Brock
Interior Design: Domini Dragoone
Moon Logo: Tim McGrath
Map Editor: Mike Morgenfeld
Cartographers: Sierra Willems, Brian Shotwell

ISBN-13: 978-1-63121-221-5

Text © 2015 by Al Argueta.
Maps © 2015 by Avalon Travel.
All rights reserved.

Some photos and illustrations are used by permission and are the property of the original copyright owners.

Front cover photo: Holy Week in Antigua © loca4motion/istockphoto.com

Title page photo: Palacio de los Capitanes Generales in Antigua © Al Argueta

All interior photos © Al Argueta, except page 2 © 123rf.com; page 3 © Elhielo | Dreamstime.com; page 5 (top) © James Crawford | Dreamstime.com; page 50 © Marcos Romero Close

Printed in the United States

About the Author

Al Argueta

At the age of three, Al Argueta first traveled to Guatemala with his father and was utterly captivated by the country's landscape and its Maya inhabitants. He would later live in Guatemala for two years, allowing him to formally learn Spanish and to experience Guatemala's culture firsthand. During summers in high school and college, Al often took a month off to travel to Guatemala, exploring its jungles, ruins, and villages.

In college, Al majored in journalism and Latin American studies, managing to squeeze in two study-abroad programs—one in Manchester and one in Maastricht—and traveled through much of Europe. After college, he interned with Costa Rica's *Tico Times*, getting his first exposure to travel writing and photography, in addition to covering then-President Bill Clinton's visit to Guatemala. Al worked briefly for a newspaper in the Virgin Islands before moving on to photography school in Hawaii. He also taught English to college students in Thailand for a time, continuing to satiate the travel bug that bit him years back.

Al now lives in Austin, Texas, where he's managed to stay put for an unprecedented eleven years. In addition to writing, he does freelance commercial and editorial photography for clients that have included *National Geographic Traveler*, *Caribbean Travel + Life*, *Condé Nast Traveler*, *Outside's GO*, and *Hemispheres*. In addition to *Moon Guatemala*, Al is also the author of *Moon Living Abroad in Guatemala*. His corporate photography clients include hotel chains such as W Hotels, Sheraton, and Marriott, in addition to several local properties in Central and South America and the United States. His website is www.alargueta.com and he can be followed on Instagram at @alargueta75. For the latest updates from Guatemala, visit Al's Facebook page at www.facebook.com/moonguatemala.

CPSIA information can be obtained at www.ICGtesting.com
Printed in the USA
LVOW01s0259250915

455610LV00002B/2/P

9 781631 212215